**How to Minister to FAMILIES
in Your Church**

HOW TO MINISTER TO

IN YOUR CHURCH

Joseph W. Hinkle and Melva J. Cook

BROADMAN PRESS
NASHVILLE, TENNESSEE

4232–24

ISBN: 0–8054–3224–8

Dewey Decimal Classification: 259

Subject Heading: CHURCH WORK WITH FAMILIES

Library of Congress Catalog Card Number: 77–82925

Printed in the United States of America

Acknowledgments

We are indebted to Myron C. Madden for consultation in the preparation of chapter 1; to Harold Bergen, Dan Kent, and Richard Waggener for their help in the preparation in chapter 6; to Jerry Brown and Henry Webb for their help in the preparation of chapters 7 and 8; to many pastors and ministers to family life who have shared experiences and materials; and to George Knight, Harold Bergen, Jerry Brown, Henry Webb, Richard Waggener, and Lee Sizemore for their contributions in evaluating and revising the manuscript.

JOE HINKLE
MELVA COOK

Contents

Contents

1
Learning to See Needs

They called her an adulteress—and she was. They called her an outcast—and she was. They pointed out that she had had five husbands and that the man with whom she was living at that time was not her husband. Their scorn was so great that she made her daily trip to the well only during the heat of the noonday to avoid meeting their eyes.

But one day was different. Jesus was there. Jesus was concerned with her needs. He offered her living water. He treated her, not as an outcast, but as a person of dignity and worth. He recognized her need.

As the contemporary minister meets persons at the well—in his study, in the sanctuary, by the wayside— he wishes for the insight of Jesus. He longs to look deep into hearts to discover needs, for he realizes that the first step in ministering to families is recognizing needs.

The minister's search for the needs of persons will begin in his own prayer life. The search will involve looking deep into his own personal life and his family life. But beyond that, how does a minister discover needs?

God has blessed us with skills and data from social scientists, psychologists, psychiatrists, physicians, and others. Church leaders now have at their disposal re-sources not known even a decade ago. They will draw from all of these disciplines as they prepare to discover needs in their congregations.

When we speak of ministry to families, we include every member of the congregation. Families come in a wide variety of styles. There was a time when a father, mother, and children were the typical family. Now the atypical family is becoming more and more typical. Family ministry must include the family of one—the never-married or formerly-married—the formerly-married with children, the couple whose children have left the nest, and the childless couple.

Just as families are not all alike in composition, they are not all alike in needs. One elderly widow may be lonely and withdrawn; another may be outgoing and living a rich, full life. One young family may be adjust-ing well to all the problems of the child-rearing years; another may be on the verge of breaking up from the frustration of coping with stress. One couple may be handling well their teenager's growing need for inde-pendence; another may be fighting a losing battle in trying to keep their parental control in spite of growing rebellion. One engaged couple may have stars in their eyes and a set of unrealistic expectations for marriage; another, just as much in love, may have better ideas of what marriage is all about. How does the church leader determine what his ministry will include for all these persons?

For married couples, the ideal may be easy to iden-tify. Isn't the goal of marriage complete intimacy on the part of each married couple? Intimacy is defined by Clinebell and Clinebell [1] as the "degree for mutual need-satisfaction within the relationship." The climate of intimacy includes the spiritual, sexual, emotional, intellectual, aesthetic, creative, recreational, work, crisis, and commitment areas of life. "Intimacy refers to two different things in marriage: (a) a close moment or period of intense sharing; (b) an ongoing quality of the relationship which is present even in times of some distance and conflict." [2]

Marriage enrichment is the united pilgrimage of a couple toward these kinds of intimacy. It is the goal toward which many church leaders wish to lead couples within their membership.

The parenting goal may be described as the development of each child to reach his potential. To achieve this goal parents must learn to accept the child's potential as it is—not as they would like for it to be. Adequate parenting involves the proper balance between guidance and independence and the wisdom to determine when and how much of the apron strings to cut. It calls for a growing maturity and acceptance on the part of the parent.

For singles the goal may be found in John 10:10: "I have come in order that you might have life—life in all its fullness" (TEV). Such meaningful life can be built only on the individual's right relationship with God and with others, as well as with self. He must view himself as a whole person of infinite worth.

Basic Needs

Basic human needs must be met if the goal is to be reached. The couple, the parent, the child, the single, the widowed, the divorced—all must be getting their needs met as persons so that they can relate as healthy family members to the close-knit fellowship in the church, the family of God.

Various psychologists have identified human needs. Although stated in different terms, most seem to include the following in addition to physical needs of food and shelter.

The first need of all persons, regardless of age, is *love.* God made us so that our own mental, emotional, and spiritual growth are dependent on our receiving love. The church is a loving group, but most congregations need to grow in the ability to experience, receive, and express love. In the circle of the church fellowship each member can give and receive loving affirmation. And part of the mission of the church is that of helping families learn how to share love in their homes.

Closely related to the need for love is the need for *acceptance.* The feeling of rejection is one which cuts deeply into one's self-esteem. The home and the church should be two areas where each person is affirmed as a person of worth.

Security—freedom from anxiety and doubt—is another basic need. The Christian faith is the basis for true security, but the ability to trust God and the ability to trust persons are closely related. Many Christians have not learned yet to rest their own faith in God. Warm expressions of affirmation given to one another at home and at church work together to bring feelings of security to each family member so that faith in God also grows.

Independence is another basic need—but one which is difficult for many parents to provide. Individuals need to take independent action as soon as they are able to act for themselves. The baby should be allowed to hold his own bottle as soon as he wants to, although he still needs cuddling which comes from Mother holding him. The toddler needs to develop some areas of independence. School years bring additional opportunities to act independently. The teenager's development will be greatly hampered if he is not allowed opportunities to assume more and more responsibility. Interdependence is learned and appreciated when and as one is comfortable handling independence responsibly.

Every individual needs a feeling of *achievement*. We must all have something which we feel we do well. Not only must parents learn to help their children to achieve, but they as adults must be achieving some life goals as they move toward realizing their own potential. Adults who receive affirmation from various sources are better able to meet the needs of their children or spouses.

Guidance and control are basic needs. Children need limits. Values and discipline are vital controls which provide comfortable guilt-free perimeters for healthy family living. To deny oneself sinful pleasures is personal discipline. To make a lifetime commitment to love a marriage partner and children is exercise of basic Christian value. Values and discipline release one's personal freedom to grow.

Beauty is another basic need. Each of us needs aesthetic appreciation in order to live life to the fullest. There is beauty in the physical world around us. There is beauty in the arts. There is beauty in the lives of those near and dear to us. God has surrounded us with beauty, but we are not always perceptive enough to enjoy it fully.

God has made man so that he must *worship* in order to live abundantly. Worship brings direction to life. "O Lord, you have always been our home./ Before you created the hills/ or brought the world into being,/ you were eternally God,/ and will be God forever" (Ps. 90:1-2, TEV) is the prayer of the worshiper.

Ministers and other family ministry leaders must first relate to their own families in ways that appropriately meet their own and their family's basic needs. Then they will be in a position to give of themselves in meeting the needs of church members.

Developmental Needs

In addition to basic human needs, persons have developmental needs. From the cradle to the grave there are cycles of development—needs and learning tasks which come to all of us. Psychologist Erik Erikson [3] identifies eight psychosocial crises common in the life cycle: basic trust *vs.* mistrust; autonomy *vs.* shame, doubt; initiative *vs.* guilt; industry *vs.* inferiority; identity *vs.* identity diffusion; intimacy *vs.* isolation; generativity *vs.* stagnation; and integrity *vs.* despair. To some degree or other, each of us experiences these crises. The mature person has learned to integrate the crises into a worthy self-image.

In *The Person* [4] Lidz describes each developmental stage in greater detail, including young adulthood, marital choices, marital adjustments, parenthood, the middle years, and old age. Each of these periods brings personal and family crises. The caring church with a comprehensive family ministry program speaks directly to these crises.

Developmental needs of the *preschool years* include

the beginnings of self-identity and self-esteem. The preschooler grows from the infant who does not recognize himself apart from his mother to the exploring, learning, growing child. He begins to recognize himself as a boy or girl.

The *childhood years* are times of further exploration and growing as the child leaves the home to enter school. He grows in his understanding of sex roles. He internalizes reactions of others to him as a person and thus forms his self-concept. He may become a Christian during this period.

The *adolescent* experiences the beginnings of breaking away and growing in independence. He is torn between the desire to be independent and the need for security and guidance from adults. His self-image may suffer if he is not allowed to develop independence in areas in which he can be responsible.

The *young adult* must make some of the most important decisions of his entire life. Those decisions relating to career, life-style, and marital state must be made. His life-style will be, to a certain extent, dependent on his career choice. Whether he chooses to marry and whom he marries will significantly affect life-style and, to a certain extent, career. The young adult who has had no experiences in making decisions in his adolescence will be greatly hampered in making wise choices in these significant areas.

Adequate studies have not been made regarding the developmental needs of the person who does not marry. Because this choice is being made more and more today, studies will likely be forthcoming. However, church leaders must be aware of this growing number of *single adults*. Life-planning seminars for single persons can provide a much-needed ministry.

Marriage adjustment is the next significant area of development for the person who marries. The early years of marriage constitute the period when two persons learn—or fail to learn—to live together. The period of parenthood usually follows. Young parents struggle with problems of rearing children, along with continuing problems of careers, marital adjustments, and everyday living.

The *middle years* represent a long-neglected area of life. This is the time when many must face the fact that lifetime goals will not be reached. Although they are at the peak of their earning years, couples may find that college expenses of their children and expenses of elderly parents often make these difficult years financially. While still worrying about their own children, many couples must make decisions regarding parents who are ill or senile. Institutional care may be the only alternative, but adults often feel guilty when they make such decisions. The middle adult years are the times of life when creative tension may be turned to the most productive and rewarding period of life.

Retirement is a critical period in the life cycle. Some have prepared for it and look forward to it. Many experience a more abundant life in retirement, while others find adjustment more difficult than they anticipated. Failing health and the necessity of giving up the home for an apartment, retirement home, or nursing home is a traumatic experience for many senior adults. Approaching death or prolonged illness may bring fears and doubts to many older persons.

Crisis Needs

In addition to developmental needs, there are crisis needs in the lives of persons in every congregation. There are definite clues by which church leaders can be led to discover needs not voluntarily shared.

When a family that has been active in church drops out, there is an underlying cause—a basic need. The reason may be a marital problem, a financial problem, a problem with children, or something else. If it is a problem that affects family life, it is a call for help to which the church should respond.

Sometimes the entire family does not drop out. One parent may continue to attend church regularly. Both parents may come but always in two cars, even when there is no apparent need for separate transportation. When Dad is more interested in the son and his activities than in Mom, and she is completely involved with her daughter, her job, or even her church responsibilities, there is reason to suspect that there may be problems in the home.

Careful attention should be given to ministering to the needs of the family as well as to helping them renew their commitment to God and their church. Church attendance is important. And the spiritual strength which comes from Christian fellowship will support a family while it is working through a serious crisis.

Grief at the death of a loved one is an obvious need for help. Leaders will realize that the need to work through grief will continue for several months after the funeral service. Going to church alone for the first time when one is accustomed to going with a mate is difficult. Probating the will, disposing of clothes and other personal effects, caring for details of insurance—all these are difficult, but perhaps not as difficult as the time when all details have been cared for. It's really over then. The first-month and the first-year anniversaries of the death are difficult days, as are birthdays, wedding anniversaries, and Christmas. Support and love are needed at these times. Help with legal and business problems is sometimes needed by widows who have no family members to provide support and assistance.

The person who cannot grieve—who will not give himself permission to grieve—also needs help. Special attention and permission to grieve should be given a person who finds it very difficult to express grief openly.

Moving is another time when persons have needs. Children and teenagers have problems in giving up school and church friends. Mom may feel that she will never like her new house as well as the old one or her new neighbors as well as the ones she left behind. Family members may feel resentment toward Dad for taking the new job or allowing himself to be transferred. The resentment may be expressed in such a way that tensions are increased. Any family moving from one community to another may have needs beyond locating a good TV repairman and doctor. Caring families from the church may help a timid family find a new Christian fellowship which will adequately bridge the gap between the friends left behind and the new relationships to be developed.

Illness may also be a cry for help. Hospital visitors who are willing to listen and who ask the right questions may discover that the real hurt is not the pain from the surgery but the ache in the heart. "How is everything in your life?" may bring forth the story of the boss or co-worker who makes the job intolerable, adultery, a breakdown in communications between parent and child, or unrealistic demands on oneself or one's family. "Let the person tell his story," says one well-known counselor. "Listen and you will discover needs." Many church leaders have a tendency to give advice and propose solutions when they could help more by encouraging the person to talk—and by listening.

Chronic aches and pains may indicate emotional stress. The person with chronic physical problems may need nothing more than someone to listen.

When terminal illness strikes a family member, it is time for caring persons in the church to stand by with loving support for the one facing death and also for the entire family. Even the most devout Christians may be afraid to die. Family members may suffer from guilt and doubts when they are under such emotional tension.

Needs of faithful church members are easily ignored. We assume that, because Mrs. Neil is at church every-time the doors are opened and because she is faithful in serving and giving, she has no crisis needs. A visit to her home by a sympathetic and understanding person and a "Tell me how everything is going in your life" may lead her to unburden her soul.

Any change in job status—either up or down—may be a critical time. The man or woman who has received a job promotion may fear failure. *What if I can't do it? What will my family and friends say if I flop?*

The spouse may have similar reactions. Job demotion or job loss affects the self-concept as well as the income. Affirmation is needed. Hurting persons need listeners and encouragement to share their feelings.

Adults are not the only ones to experience crises. The little leaguer who strikes out in the crucial game may feel that life is not worth living. The teenager who doesn't have a date for the big event of the year, the college graduate who didn't get the job, the guy who didn't get the girl, or the girl who didn't get the guy—all these needs are special. The student who didn't get the scholarship may not need help any more than the one who did—but who fears failure. Families may or may not recognize and meet one another's needs. Sometimes a sympathetic and understanding Sunday School teacher or church staff member can be the answer.

In large churches, there may be distinctive groups who need and want specialized help. Families where one parent travels, for example; parents of retarded, deaf, or accelerated children; stepparents, expectant parents, and parents whose occupations greatly affect family life may be in need of family ministry.

Organizational leaders may be trained to look for symptoms of needs and to share with church leaders. Information shared through concern is redemptive. Gossip shared for any reason is damaging, hurtful, and unchristian.

As the church leader discovers where his people are in their family lives and where God wants them to be in order to live abundantly, he sees needs. Meeting these needs becomes the family ministry program of the church.

Notes

1. Charlotte H. and Howard J. Clinebell, *The Intimate Marriage* (New York: Harper and Row, 1970), p. 1. Used by permission.

2. Ibid., p. 32. Used by permission.

3. Erik Erikson, *Identity and the Life Cycle* (New York: International Universities Press, Inc., 1959.

4. Theodore Lidz, *The Person* (New York: Basic Books, Inc., 1968).

For Further Study

Erikson, Erik. *Identity and the Life Cycle.* New York: International Universities Press, Inc., 1959.

Gadpaille, Warren. *The Cycles of Sex.* New York: Charles Scribner's Sons, 1975.

Lidz, Theodore. *The Person.* New York: Basic Books, Inc., 1968.

Sheehy, Gail. *Passages.* New York: E. P. Dutton and Company, Inc., 1976.

Sherrill, Lewis. *The Struggle of the Soul.* New York: Macmillan Company, 1951.

2
The Scope of Family Ministry

What is family ministry? What happens between the discovery of need and the reaching of the goal?

Family ministry is caring. In a sense, everything that a church does could be called ministry (service), and everyone is a family unit or a part of a family unit. Evangelism, outreach, education, and worship—all enrich the lives of persons and families. However, we usually do not define family ministry with such a broad scope as to include those functions.

Ministry has been defined as a loving response to need made in the name of Jesus. Any Christian service related to needs which affect family living may be called *family ministry.*

In the light of its own concept of its mission, each church must determine the extent of its own ministry. It may choose to minister only to its members and immediate prospects, or it may see its role as providing ministry to any persons in its geographical area who want or need ministry.

Redemption is the central theme of Christianity and is the central theme of family ministry. The attitude of the church should be that shown by Jesus toward the woman taken in adultery (John 8:1–11). He loved her. He forgave her. He told her to sin no more. In no way did he condone her actions, but he did not condemn her as a person. The same spirit was shown in his conversation with the woman at the well (John 4:5-25). Other Jewish men would not have spoken to her, but Jesus was more concerned with what she could become than what she had been.

Churches need loving, caring support systems for all persons, regardless of those persons' sins. Each church needs places for all persons in its life and work, places where each can feel comfortable, loved, wanted, forgiven, and challenged to grow. And we have a responsibility to those on the outside—those, like the woman at the well, who are outcasts.

Preventive Ministry

Family ministry is not limited in scope to those on the brink of crises. It is for everyone. It includes opportunities for life enrichment and for preventive measures in relation to family crises. It includes family life education. Family members need opportunities to grow. Within the context of the church, growth groups can be provided to develop skills needed in family living. These may be communication skills, parenting skills, money management skills, and coping skills. Sometimes these skills may be developed within the program organizations of the church; sometimes they will be featured in special activities such as retreats, seminars, and conferences. Growth is positive action for *preventing* marriage and family breakdown. Family life education is a major part of the church's opportunities for growth and personal and spiritual enrichment.

Jesus provided growth or preventive ministry in his last days with his disciples. Since he knew what was ahead, his concern was for them: "Let not your heart be troubled. . . . And I will pray the Father, and he shall give you another Comforter, ... And now I have told you before it come to pass, that, when it is come to pass, ye might believe" (John 14:1,16,29).

One area of preventive ministry is premarital guidance, and closely related is premarital counseling. Preparation for marriage doesn't begin when the rings are purchased. Values, ideals, and standards are set in the early years. Education for marriage should begin in preschool years, with the good example of loving parents and the positive teachings of the church. A healthy self-concept is essential in a healthy marriage. The preschool years are extemely important in the development of the self-concept. Sex education also begins in the preschool years. Consideration for the wholesome feelings of maleness and femaleness and rights of others are part of healthy human development. Personal and spiritual wholeness are thus a concern of the church.

Elementary school and youth years are times for establishment of values. Sex education in these years must be related to Christian values to provide a wholesome basis for Christian marriage. Children and youth often learn the *facts* in school; they need to internalize *values* through the teachings and examples of parents at home and leaders at church.

Youth groups are frequently given opportunities to learn about family budgeting and money management. This experience is excellent training. Opportunities for growth in self-understanding contribute to better marriages. Training in communication skills is also important during these years, not only to meet present needs but also as preparation for marriage.

Singleness is an option which more and more people are choosing. Young people need to understand that either option is open to them and that in either case their lives can be completely in the will of God.

Through family life education all members of the family may be given opportunities and experiences leading to the enrichment of family life in the here and now. Such experiences in communication are important, especially communication between husbands and wives and between parents and youth. Learning to communicate—to discover and express hidden and denied feelings—is one of the most enriching experiences for any relationship. Adequate communication enables families to resolve conflict in personally rewarding manners for everyone involved. As families learn how to look at their problems, to discover and evaluate possible solutions, and to make decisions which are best for all involved, they will develop as competent families.

Education in parenting is a vital part of the church's family ministry. Understanding the growth needs of children in general, and of each individual child in particular, is not an easy assignment. Parents need help. Some parents tend to use the child to meet the parent's own needs. Other parents are concerned with helping the child to be himself. Some parents will allow the child to do exactly as he pleases, believing that they are making him happy. Others recognize the need for guidelines and discipline. To some parents, discipline is punishment for wrongdoing; to more mature parents, discipline is more likely to be guidance and restrictions to encourage self-discipline

Marriage enrichment, a fairly new system for marital growth, is a means of making good marriages better and of fostering growth in marriage relationships.

Preaching can be a method of positive family ministry. When sermons relate to everyday living and to personal and family growth, lives will be enriched. Lay persons come to church seeking help with personal and family hurts. Many burdens are lifted and problems resolved in worship experiences when a sensitive pastor has carefully opened the practical meaning of some biblical passage. Preaching which relates to family life needs is a vital part of family enrichment. That kind of ministry may well prevent family breakdown.

Crisis Ministry

In addition to positive growth ministry, church leaders must help families as they face serious crises. For many years churches have provided food, child care, transportation, and other ministries in times of death, serious illness, or natural disasters among church families. Women's groups or Sunday School classes have often performed this service. Often deacons provide crisis ministry through The Deacon Family Ministry Plan (see chapter 8).

Crisis ministry is vital in a caring church. Crises come to everyone, and churches demonstrate their love and concern at such times. Jesus gave us the example. Although he must have been tired after an exciting and exhausting experience in the synagogue, he was ready to help when he went to Peter's home and found the mother-in-law sick with a fever. When a ruler of the synagogue came with a request for Jesus' help in the healing of his daughter, Jesus responded. Homes must have been different after Jesus demonstrated his concern for the blind, the lame, the possessed, the hungry, the sorrowing. He always showed the most tender concern for suffering of any kind.

In times of serious crisis the immediate need may be for the simple cup of cold water offered in Jesus' name. Sometimes words of encouragement or acts of kindness may be used miraculously in healing wounds.

There is a need for a broad and carefully planned crisis ministry, however. Lay leaders have the potential expertise for providing the needed ministry when a family is about to break up, when the divorce has been granted, when a teenage daughter is pregnant, when a child runs away from home, when a youth is on drugs, when a widow has not worked through her grief a year after the funeral, when a marriage partner is having an affair, when a woman has been raped, or in many other crisis situations. A training program may be provided to sensitize and equip church members for taking care of one another in times of crisis. Persons can learn the *how* and *when* for giving reassurance, prayers, and support. They also need to know how to make referrals when the situation calls for professional help not available in the church.

Children and youth especially need loving ministry at the time of crisis—and sometimes they are overlooked. When a parent dies, a child often feels responsible. Reaction to divorce or separation may be similar; the child or even the youth may feel that it is his fault that the parents have broken up. Because of their own grief, parents may not be able to give the support their children need from them. Church members may be trained to help.

In summary, these may be stated as the areas of family ministry in the local church:

• To help family members learn to communicate with one another and to understand and solve family problems

• To help couples enrich their relationship

• To help parents to understand their children and their needs and to learn to meet their needs in a mature way

• To help those who are divorced to find acceptance in the church and to grow in their personal lives

• To help single parents understand and cope with problems they encounter in rearing children without mates

• To help all singles and senior adults to grow in self-understanding and to assume responsibility for making their lives worthwhile

• To provide opportunities for single adults and for senior adults to form wholesome friendships and to enrich their lives

• To help families in times of crisis.

If the church has truly become a *koinonia*—a fellowship of grace—members will care. They will express their concern and love to fellow members at times when such affirmation is needed. "Help carry one another's burdens, and in this way you will obey the law of Christ" (Gal. 6:2, TEV).

For Further Study

Hulme, William E. *The Pastoral Care of Families*. New York: Abingdon Press, 1962.

3
A Theology of Family Ministry

Growing numbers of ministers are becoming very concerned about family problems in our land. These leaders are studying the Bible from the viewpoint of seeking to know more about the place of the family in God's plan. Ideas presented here may be of help to the minister in developing his own theology regarding the family and the ministry of the church to the family.

A Theology of Personhood

Since families are made up of persons, we begin with a consideration of personhood. Psalm 8 points to the value which God places on persons:

"When I look at the sky, which you have made, / at the moon and the stars, which you set in their places— / what is man, that you think of him; / mere man, that you care for him? / Yet you made him inferior only to yourself, you crowned him with glory and honor. / You appointed him ruler over everything you made; / you placed him over all creation; / sheep and cattle, and the wild animals too; / the birds and the fish / and the creatures in the seas" (Ps. 8:3–8, TEV).

God created man; God loved him; God prepared a way for his redemption; God's Son died for him; God is preparing a place for him. Man is important to God.

The fact that God made man a free moral agent is a vital part of our theology of man. From the beginning God wanted to live in a free and loving relationship with man. Yet he gave man the ability to make his own choices regarding that relationship. Man sinned. Regardless of sin, God wanted man to experience the fullness of life by restoring fellowship through redeeming forgiveness in Jesus Christ. But God left the way open for man to accept or reject that redemption. God made every man free and, therefore, responsible for himself. Although parents are responsible for the nurture and care of their offspring during childhood, the time comes when parents must let go. Parents and church leaders must accept the fact that all persons become responsible for their own personal decisions related to self, others, and God. Leaders seek to influence, not to control. God sets an example in that he does not attempt to manipulate persons. He continues to love and to care, but not to coerce.

Though he is a sinner, man's worth comes from the fact that he is created capable of having fellowship with God. Persons are worth every concern offered by the church.

By New Testament standards, the worth of woman equals the worth of man. Each is judged on his/her own merit; and, in God's sight, there is no *male* or *female,* but *persons* (see Gal. 3:28).

A workable theology of personhood for the family minister may be based on his response to these questions: Of what worth is a person? How much right does each individual have to choose his own destiny?

A Theology of the Family

The establishment of the family is recorded in the first chapter of the Bible. "So God created man in his own image; in the image of God he created him; male and female he created them. God blessed them and said to them, 'Be fruitful and increase, fill the earth and subdue it' " (Gen. 1:27–28, NEB). The second chapter enlarges on these details: "Then the Lord God said, 'It is not good for the man to be alone. I will provide a partner for him' " (Gen. 2:18, NEB). "That is why a man leaves his father and mother and is united to his wife, and the two become one flesh" (Gen. 2:24, NEB). These passages state God's ideal, value, and sanctity of the family. The family is God's creation. It had his blessing from the beginning.

The Old Testament has much to say about the sanctity of the home. God intended that monogamous companions should fulfill each other and rear and teach their children the same values. In Hebrew history we find that alternate family styles emerged but were not sanctioned by God. Adultery was punishable by death (Lev. 20:10). Polygamy was common, but there was no biblical support for it.

In New Testament times, monogamy had become a fairly standard practice. Perhaps it was due to tragic experiences in the lives of many polygamist families, as well as God's unfolding revelation, that the ideal of one man and one woman came to be accepted as the norm.

Hebrew society was basically patriarchal. Women were *things* rather than persons and had few rights.

They were, in most cases, not companions and help-mates but childbearers. While some other societies in history have been matriarchal, Hebrew men owned all property, made all decisions, and ruled their households with an iron hand.

The marriage relationship, however, was so respected that honeymooners were given special privileges: "When a man is newly married, he shall not be liable for military service or any other public duty. He shall remain at home exempt from service for one year and enjoy the wife he has taken" (Deut. 24:5, NEB).

Marriage was greatly desired. If an unmarried person died, a form of marriage ceremony was part of the burial service. Prophetic and symbolic references were based on genuine respect for marriage: "And in that day seven women shall take hold of one man, saying, We will eat our own bread, and wear our own apparel: only let us be called by thy name, to take away our reproach" (Isa. 4:1). "And she went with her companions, and bewailed her virginity upon the mountains" (Judg. 11:38). The prophet Jeremiah told of a forthcoming day of sadness when the voices of the bride and bridegroom would no longer be heard in the land (Jer. 7:34).

Jesus supported family life by attending a wedding (John 2) and by numerous illustrations based on the idea of marriage (see Matt. 25:1-6; 22:12). In Matthew 19:4-6 he called attention to an Old Testament concept: "Have ye not read, . . . For this cause shall a man leave father and mother, and shall cleave to his wife: and they twain shall be one flesh? Wherefore they are no more twain, but one flesh. What therefore

God hath joined together, let not man put asunder."

Jesus' standards for sexual behavior were the highest. But his attitude toward those who had not lived up to those standards was redemptive rather than punitive. To the woman at the well he said, "If thou knewest the gift of God, and who it is that saith to thee, Give me to drink; thou wouldest have asked of him, and he would have given thee living water" (John 4:10). To the woman taken in adultery, he said, "Neither do I condemn thee: go, and sin no more" (John 8:11).

Paul used the marriage relationship to illustrate the union of Christ with his church. However, he seemed to be opposed to marriage in 1 Corinthians 7; but this passage was probably based on the belief that Christ's return was imminent. Paul indicated that this idea was not from the Lord, but was his own belief.

About nine years after writing the letter to Corinth, Paul wrote his letter to the church at Ephesus. By this time he seems to have matured in his view of marriage. No longer was it the least desirable option; it had become so sacred that it could symbolize the relationship between Christ and the church.

The writer of Hebrews also supported marriage: "Marriage is honourable in all, and the bed undefiled" (Heb. 13:4).

The family minister's theology must deal with the matter of authority in the home. There are those who take Ephesians 5:22–24 to mean that the husband should have complete control over his wife. There are others who read that passage in light of "Submit yourselves to one another because of your reverence for Christ" (Eph. 5:21, TEV) and "A man should fulfill his duty as a husband, and a woman should fulfill her duty as a wife, and each should satisfy the other's needs. A wife is not the master of her own body, but her husband is; in the same way the husband is not the master of his own body, but his wife is" (1 Cor. 7: 3–4, TEV). Paul told us, "So there is no difference between Jews and Gentiles, between slaves and free men, between men and women; you are all one in union with Christ Jesus" (Gal. 3:28, TEV).

The status of women in New Testament times and the status of women today makes a difference in the application of these passages. Women who were uneducated, could not own property, vote, or speak to a man (even a relative) on the street were quite different from today's women who are often well educated, financially independent, and responsible citizens. Christian marriage in its ideal form takes on a relationship pattern as the diagram below.

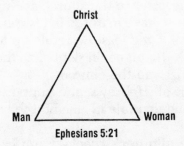

If Christ is the head, man and woman become equal partners, each subject to Christ and controlled by his love. Neither partner is to dominate the other. Each partner has a personal commitment to Christ and to the spouse. They are free in Christ to relate to each other in ways that meet each other's needs. Further, they are free to work out the roles which each will perform in the relationship.

When Paul talked about marriage role relationships in Ephesians 5:21–33, he began with mutual commitment to Christ. The wife was taught to maintain a strong commitment to her husband, whose leadership role in the marriage was to be like that of Jesus Christ, who became a servant (Eph. 5:22–23). Philippians 2:5–8 gives an insightful picture of the kind of leader Christ was. That style of leadership is appropriate for a Christian husband, as well as for a pastor or a person in any vocation. A wife of any era in history can relate to that kind of leadership with integrity and respect. There is nothing in the Bible that permits either marriage partner to dominate the other. There is strong teaching for mutual respect, commitment, and love. The husband is to love his wife *as* Christ loved the church (Eph. 5:25).

Much has been said about the influence of Christianity on the status of women. In the traditional morning prayer of Hebrew men, they thanked God that they had not been born Gentiles or women. Devout Jewish men would not speak to women on the street—even their own wives.

Greek wives in New Testament times were even more oppressed than Jewish women. Wives seldom left their homes, never ate meals with their husbands, and were in no way companions. Courtesans and prostitutes were socially higher than wives.

Prostitution was an integral part of worship in Greek temples. When Paul gave his instructions to women regarding their dress and conduct, he was admonishing them not to act like prostitutes. If women had dressed elaborately, cut their hair, or spoken in the church services in certain Greek cities, Greeks would have assumed that these women were prostitutes and that prostitution was a part of Christian worship. Paul did not seem to be giving principles for all times, but rather offering specific guidelines for appropriate Christian behavior for that situation.

When men and women are equal partners, both women and men are liberated. No longer is the man solely responsible for his household—all family members are responsible. He is not responsible for the thoughts and actions of his wife; she is his partner, not his property.

A Theology of Divorce

The family minister must come to grips with the question of divorce; the rate of marital breakup is constantly rising. It is important how one views persons involved in a divorce crisis.

Jesus was clear in Matthew 19:4-5 and Mark 10: 2-9 that God's plan is for marriage to last until death. That is God's ideal. Because men and women are not perfect, they do not live up to God's ideal in any area of life.

Sometimes the marriage relationship deteriorates until it disintegrates. Many theologians and marriage counselors believe that when a marriage relationship has ended, there is no benefit, and often a great deal of emotional harm, in continuing the outward form. People—Christians as well as non-Christians—make mistakes. A broken marriage is a crisis and brings pain to those involved. But there are times when the crisis and pain are less than if the troubled marriage were to continue.

Couples are sometimes told that there will be no marital problems if they stay in fellowship with God.

However, a right relationship with God does not automatically make one able to relate perfectly or to live harmoniously with a spouse in marriage. Devout Christians do not automatically learn to communicate. The devout man may neglect his wife emotionally just as any other man. The devout may suffer from sexual frustration or inability to handle emotional conflict. Thus marital problems may come even to the devout. Often marriage partners who have problems may begin to doubt their Christianity. They may think that these problems are indications that they are not genuinely saved.

Since about one marriage out of four is a remarriage, remarriage after divorce is another part of this thorny question. Mark 10:11–12 seems to say that under no circumstances is remarriage after divorce acceptable, while Matthew 19:9 may be interpreted to mean that unfaithfulness of one marriage partner may leave the other free to remarry. Each church leader must seek the leadership of the Holy Spirit in forming his own theology in this area.

Remarriage is not the unpardonable sin. A Christian may struggle through a divorce following an unfortunate marriage and experience God's grace. That former marriage has died. Many sincere Christians have felt that God led them into a truly Christian marriage after they had experienced divorce. The church and its leaders will want to help couples make a success of the second marriage. In *The Right to Remarry,* Dwight Hervey Small says:

> The justification for remarriage in God's sight must arise
> from the reality of grace. Remarriage is always related
> to the renewing grace of God, which meets a person in

his or her failure and grants another chance . . . . Remarriage for some may be a redemptive fulfillment, a new opportunity to reverse the former failure, to fulfill the order of Creation in a particular marriage, to seek an enduring, Christ-controlled marriage. Where divorce has been judged necessary for the well-being of the parties involved, the divorced person may enter a marriage so centered in Christ's love and purpose that any divorce of that marriage would be impossible. In a renewed opportunity, such a spiritually motivated person will demonstrate the intrinsically indissoluable nature of a truly Christian marriage—and this to the glory of God. Remarriage can be redemptive! [1]

Some Bible scholars believe that Jesus' references in Matthew 5:31–32; 19:3–9; Mark 10:11–12; and Luke 16:18 relate to conditions for divorce rather than remarriage. They believe that Jesus was saying that it is wrong for a person to divorce his spouse *in order to* marry someone else. In *An Open Book to the Christian Divorcee,* Roger H. Crook says: "We are probably reading too much into what he said if we interpret this passage as a prohibition of remarriage. It is entirely consistent with what he said to assume that a marriage which has been ended, whether by divorce or by death of one of the marriage partners, would not in itself constitute a barrier to the contracting of a new marriage." [2]

Some ministers do not agree with either Small or Crook and do not perform marriage ceremonies for persons who have been divorced. That is their prerogative. Whatever the minister's attitude toward remarriage, however, the ideal relationship of the divorced person and his church should be one of love and redemption. The divorced person has not lived up to God's ideal for marriage, but neither has anyone else in the church lived up to all the ideals and values of God.

A Theology of Parenting

Can a married couple live a full life without having children? Is a desire not to have children based on selfishness? Is the use of contraceptive wrong? Is abortion wrong? What responsibility do parents have in bringing up children? Must the mother always do the child rearing, or does an equal part of the responsibility belong to the father? How does a parent draw the line between responsibility to himself and responsibility to his child?

Like most contemporary questions, these are thorny. Direct answers are not all found in the Bible; the theologian must use biblical principles to work out his own answers.

Children were highly regarded by Hebrews. To be barren was the greatest curse known for women. To have many sons was a man's greatest dream, and children were considered to be God's greatest blessing. Rachel said to Jacob, "Give me children, or else I die" (Gen. 30:1). Hannah was willing to give her child to God if only he would give her a son.

At the present time, this attitude toward big families has changed significantly. The high cost of living makes the support of a large family difficult. The world food shortage, brought about because of the population explosion, makes small families seem to be the unselfish, rather than the selfish, reality. Many couples today are choosing to have no children or to limit the size of their families. Such choices may be selfish or unselfish, depending on motivation.

The Levitical law made responsibility for religious education of children clear. The familiar "Gather the people together, men, and women, and children, and thy stranger that is within thy gates, that they may hear, and that they may learn, and fear the Lord your God, and observe to do all the words of this law" (Deut. 31:12) refers to a one-in-seven years' assembly (Deut. 31:10). Obviously, that could not have been the total of religious education; we conclude that parents, rather than the religious community, were responsible for such training. "And these words, which I command thee this day, shall be in thine heart: and thou shalt teach them diligently unto thy children, and shalt talk of them when thou sittest in thine house, and when thou walkest by the way, and when thou liest down, and when thou risest up" (Deut. 6:6–7) was well known by Hebrew fathers. The Hebrew child grew up in this environment where religion and religious conversation were a part of everyday life.

The writer of Proverbs instructed parents to "Train up a child in the way he should go: and when he is old, he will not depart from it" (Prov. 22:6). Children were admonished to respond positively to their parents' teachings: "My son, hear the instruction of thy father, and forsake not the law of thy mother" (Prov. 1:8).

Paul was training the Ephesians in parenting and family relationships when he wrote: "Children, obey your parents in the Lord: for this is right. Honour thy father and mother; which is the first commandment with promise; that it may be well with thee, and thou mayest live long on the earth. And, ye fathers, provoke not your children to wrath: but bring them up in the nurture and admonition of the Lord" (Eph. 6:1–3). Paul gave children rights—fathers were not to rule so sternly that children rebelled.

However the minister states his theology of parenting, he cannot avoid giving the role of parents a priority in his ministry. The future depends upon it.

A Theology of Single Adults

Single adults, other than widows, seem to have been unknown in Old Testament times. Polygamy was practiced and women married very early. Marriage was so much a part of everyday life, even in New Testament times, that it was taken for granted.

However, Paul's references in 1 Corinthians 7 indicate that there were single men and women in the church at Corinth. Paul may never have been married. He urged the unmarried not to marry so that they might serve God more effectively. Perhaps because he believed that Jesus was to return immediately, Paul felt that all Christians should devote all their time to serving Christ.

Widows were common because of the high death rate, and both Old and New Testaments have much to say about the responsibility for their welfare. "Ye shall not afflict any widow, or fatherless child" (Ex. 22:22); "Thou shalt not . . . take a widow's raiment to pledge" (Deut. 24:17); and "When thou cuttest down thine harvest in thy field, and hast forgot a sheaf in the field, thou shalt not go again to fetch it: it shall be for the stranger, for the fatherless, and for the widow: that the Lord thy God may bless thee in all the work of thine hands" (Deut. 24:19).

Jesus rebuked the Pharisees for their mistreatment of widows (Matt. 23:14). James seemed to call for ministry other than the meeting of physical needs: "Pure religion and undefiled before God and the Father is this, To visit the fatherless and widows in their affliction" (Jas. 1:27). Paul said, "If any man or woman that believeth have widows, let them relieve them, and let not the church be charged; that it may relieve them that are widows indeed" (1 Tim. 5:16). The seven were appointed to minister daily to widows in the membership of the Jerusalem church (Acts 6:1–6). Because employment for women was almost unknown, it was necessary for churches to provide support for widows who had no near relatives to care for them. Otherwise, these widows would have starved. Clearly the community of faith was charged with physical responsibility for widows in their midst, a ministry never to be forgotten.

Although marriage was created by God and is within his will, there is no biblical basis for beliefs that the single person is incomplete. Both Jesus and Paul were single. Matthew 19 and 1 Corinthians 7 provide assurances that the single life can be within the will of God. The person who is not complete and well integrated before marriage will likely be no more complete and well integrated after marriage.

The minister's theology of single adulthood must relate to the relative worth of a single person and a married person. His response will determine whether singles become a part of the *koinonia* of the church.

A Theology of the Aging

In the Old Testament, especially, the aged were honored and revered. As long as a man lived, he was head of the clan. His children were subject to him, regardless of their ages, as witnessed in the story of Jacob sending his sons to Egypt for food. "Honor thy father and thy mother" was not a commandment given to young children. "You shall rise in the presence of grey hairs, give honour to the aged, and fear your God" (Lev. 19:32, NEB).

The writer of Proverbs had much to say about respect for old age. "A wise man [not child] sees the reason for his father's correction" (Prov. 13:1, NEB). "Grey hair is a crown of glory" (Prov. 16:31, NEB). "If a man reviles father and mother, his lamp will go out when darkness comes" (Prov. 20:20, NEB). "The glory of young men is their strength, the dignity of old men their grey hairs" (Prov. 20:29, NEB). "Do not despise your mother when she is old" (Prov. 23:22, NEB). "The eye that mocks a father or scorns a mother's old age will be plucked out by magpies or eaten by the vulture's young" (Prov. 30:17, NEB). Respect and love for the aging is clearly the plan of God. How respect and love can best be expressed in the complex society of today is one of the most difficult questions we face. The minister's theology of old age will largely determine what place the aging have in the life and work of the church.

The minister's theology regarding personhood, marriage, family, divorce, parenting, singlehood, and the aging will have an impact on the fellowship of the church. A growing interest and expanding ministry to families in the church may significantly enrich the life and work of the church as a whole. A family ministry focus can enrich the church's outreach and evangelistic efforts as well as strengthen educational and spiritual growth of its members.

Notes

1. Dwight Hervey Small, *The Right to Remarry* (Old Tappan: Fleming H. Revell Co., 1975), pp. 183, 185. Used by permission.
2. Roger H. Crook, *An Open Book to the Christian Divorcee* (Nashville: Broadman Press, 1974), p. 145. Used by permission.

For Further Study

Barclay, William. *The Letters of the Galatians and Ephesians.* Philadelphia: Westminster Press, 1958.
Hulme, William E. *The Pastoral Care of Families.* New York: Abingdon Press, 1962.

4
Organizing for Family Ministry

Most churches have an organization—the Sunday School—for Bible teaching. Many have choirs for teaching and performing music, groups for training leaders and members, and informal classes for studying missions.

Because there is no single organization in the church which one joins to receive and learn how to give family ministry, there is often a problem in finding handles to set this program in motion. Often no one is given the family ministry responsibility, and thus nothing is done. There is a variety of ways to organize for family ministry; several alternatives are proposed.

Professional Leadership

Large churches may consider the employment of a family life minister to lead the family ministry program. (Other job titles such as minister of pastoral care or minister to families may be used.) The family life minister should be a person sensitive to family life needs. College work in psychology and sociology and seminary work in pastoral ministry, counseling, and religious education are desirable.

The family life minister will direct a program of family life education as well as give certain hours each week to counseling by appointment. Group counseling (for such groups as persons in marriage crises, single parents, divorced persons, widows, or engaged couples) may be scheduled at other times.

He will normally be responsible for scheduling, planning, and directing parent meetings, marriage enrichment activities, Christian Home Week, and senior adult and single adult activities. (In many instances he will not personally preside at the meeting, but he is responsible for developing content and/or enlisting program personnel.) He may lead the church in mission action related to the family, such as work with juveniles in trouble, prisoners, alcoholics, unwed mothers, and runaway youth. Or these activities may be assigned to the minister of missions if the church has such.

In very large churches, there may be a minister to single adults and a minister to senior adults to handle those areas of work.

Although the family life minister will be responsible for the program, he will want to involve as many people as possible in the planning process. The program must meet the needs and interests of the people if it is to succeed. The work will be coordinated with the total church program through the church council. Job descriptions in this area are found at the end of this chapter.

Combination Staff Position

The church that cannot add a family life minister to its staff may assign the duties to an assistant pastor, a minister of education, or some other staff member. The pastor may assume as much of the work of the family life minister as his schedule permits.

By far the largest number of churches will not have a family life minister. Many will not have staff members other than the pastor. In such churches, the pastor may lead the church council or some other group to study all phases of family ministry, to enumerate jobs to be done (such as those in the sample job descriptions found on pp. 52–57), and to make their own job descriptions. The pastor may indicate which of the duties he feels that he can assume. Other tasks may be assigned to a committee or lay director.

Committee or Lay Director

In some churches a family life committee may be the best way to conduct the program. The committee can be responsible for assuming much of the work suggested for the family life minister. They may enlist lay persons or, in some instances, staff members from the church to direct the various activities. They will report to the church council for evaluation and approval of the schedule and plans.

Some churches provide recreation buildings in which the family members may, together as families or each person with his age group, participate in recreation in a Christian setting. Recently there has been a trend toward calling these buildings "Family Life Centers." The minister of recreation may be called family life director. This is a misnomer unless the director is trained in family life education and counseling and assumes the responsibilities covered in the job descriptions at the end of this chapter. A recreation building can be either a plus or a minus for family life, so calling it a family life center may not be wise.

A lay family life director or chairman may be used

instead of a committee. One person may be responsible for planning (with as much input from others as possible) the program and enlisting leaders for each activity. The church council may serve as the coordinating and approval group.

Ministry to Singles

Within the last decade, work with single adults in the local church has made tremendous progress. The church staff position of minister to single adults is becoming more common. Sample job descriptions for this position are to be found at the end of this chapter.

In working with singles, it is important to keep in mind that they are adults who can be, and need to be, responsible for themselves. This means that their programs in the church need to be as indigenous as possible. Single adults will respond at the point of their own felt need and will stay involved in any program they feel is theirs.

Another point to remember is that singles need not always be segregated. Participation in total church programs is more healthy than becoming a "little church" all their own. The attitude of the church toward singles will determine whether they are willing to participate.

The *single adult council* has proved to be a most effective way of conducting a coordinated program for singles in many churches. It is one of the best ways to involve singles themselves in planning their programs. The council should be made up of representatives of organizational units. Organizational leaders of singles may be represented on the council, but the majority should be singles themselves. Very large churches may choose to have a single young adult council and a single median adult council.

The council may elect a chairman, vice-chairman, and secretary. Usually a staff member will serve as sponsor of the group, but a lay person may serve in that capacity. If the church has a family life minister, he may be assigned the responsibility.

The council is responsible to the church for planning, conducting, and evaluating activities that involve the entire age span represented by the council. For example, if there are two singles' departments in Sunday School, class or department activities would not be the concern of the council. However, when activities for the entire membership of both departments (or for subgroups—such as single parents or divorced persons from both departments) are planned, the council is responsible.

Activities may be held as often as needed. Activities should be varied in purpose. Some will be solely for fellowship while others will provide counseling and/or education; some will provide help for single parents; some will provide help for divorced or widowed persons; and some will help singles cope with everyday problems. Some will be service opportunities designed to lead singles to share and serve.

Some larger churches have something every night, while others cannot provide such a comprehensive program. There may be recreational activities two nights a week, seminars one night, mission or service projects one night, and fellowship or worship activities another. Not everyone will participate in all activities; some will be restricted to specific target groups. Churches with recreational buildings may provide handball, volleyball, tennis, softball, swimming, and other sports on a regular basis. Other groups may be more interested in table games or in just being together for informal visiting. Some programs include coffeehouses.

Seminars may be held weekly. Singles are interested in learning many things, and larger churches may be able to offer a wide variety of learning opportunities. Some meet on Wednesday evening between dinner and the prayer meeting hour. Others meet after the prayer meeting hour. Other evenings may be more convenient; meet when the singles can attend.

Service activities may become a part of the program at times. Singles may provide a tutoring program or coaching staff for children in a ghetto area. They may visit lonely people in nursing homes, shopping for them, fixing their hair, or writing letters for them. They may paint a building used by a mission or give a party for children in an orphanage. They may clean up and fix up the home of an elderly and needy church member. In cooperation with Sunday School leaders, they may conduct Backyard Bible Clubs in early hours of long summer evenings. They may make mission tours, using their vacations to serve churches or missions in pioneer areas. Coordinate projects with other mission action or ministry activities of the church.

Retreats or camps may be planned during the year. Although fellowship is an important part, a specific objective will usually be stated for program content. For example, one retreat might have the theme "Growth Through Prayer Life" while another might be on "Learning to Care."

Ministry to Senior Adults

Much that has been said about organization for single adults also applies to senior adults. They, too, can and should be responsible for themselves. They, too, should not always be segregated. Their lives are enriched by experiences with persons of all ages.

Senior adults are capable of planning their own programs. A church staff person may serve as a resource person to assist as needed, but involvement of as many persons as possible in planning their own programs is desirable.

Senior adults may use the council form of organization, with representatives of Sunday School classes and other church program organizations making up the council. Other churches may have a weekday senior adult group, with members composed of those in church program organizations, or, in some instances, any senior adult in the community who wishes to participate.

A few larger churches are providing ministers to senior adults as members of the church staff. A job description for such a staff member is included at the end of this chapter.

Intergenerational Activities

Many church leaders feel that churches need more intergenerational activities. Older couples, young couples and their children, single parents and their children, and never-marrieds may never cross paths in large churches. Intergenerational activities provide opportunities for enrichment of each group through contact with the others.

Family clustering is one way of meeting this need. Sometimes called the extended family program, this movement is spreading slowly; but those who have become involved are enthusiastic.

One church began with two hundred adults who had

volunteered to participate by being divided into groups of about fourteen each. Each group contained married couples with children, married couples without children, and singles. No attempt was made to select persons of like background or interests.

A leader (who had received three months of training) was assigned to each group. Leaders were to serve as facilitators, not directors or decision makers. They had been instructed to make their role unnecessary as soon as possible.

Members of each cluster agreed to participate for three months and then to determine whether the group would continue. Group members were to keep in touch with one another, to help one another when help was needed, to meet together to share meals, to enjoy one another's company, to worship, and to become a family. Each group determined when and how often and where it would meet.

Some families met weekly, some twice a month, some monthly, and some irregularly. The program is limited only by the creativity of family members; the church does not attempt to direct activities.

A Patchwork Family by Mark and Mary Frances Henry was released by Broadman in April of 1978. This book will be helpful for church leaders interested in an intergenerational approach to family ministry.

Sample Job Descriptions

The following job descriptions are in the form used by various churches and, therefore, are not consistent in format.

Minister of Counseling and Mission Coordinator
Report to: Minister of Education and Administration

Basic Functions: To provide a counseling program for the membership of the church and to coordinate the mission activities of the church.

Responsibilities:
I. Counseling Responsibilities
   1. Provide personal counseling
      (1) Counsel with individuals and families
      (2) Lead or provide leadership for group therapy sessions
      (3) Visit in situations with family difficulty
      (4) Be acquainted with resources and referrals
   2. Provide family life education
      (1) Develop plans with church staff and councils
      (2) Recommend resources and available leadership
      (3) Serve as resource person or leader as requested
   3. Involve membership in ministry to families
      (1) Work with pastor in leading members to commit themselves to concept of "every Christian a minister"
      (2) Work through appropriate channels to provide ministry by members to families in need
      (3) Assist in planning and/or conducting needed training
II. Missions Coordination
   1. Discover community needs appropriate for ministry by various church groups or individuals
      (1) With appropriate organizations, deter-

mine resources required by each possible
project
   (2) Make recommendations to missions committee as to feasibility of mission projects
2. Involve membership in ministry/missions action projects
   (1) Work with pastor in leading congregation
to commit themselves to ministry concept
   (2) Work with appropriate channels to discover and enlist individuals and groups
suitable for a ministry project
   (3) Develop plans with church and/or organizational councils for training ministers
   (4) Oversee work of ministry groups as
required.

Minister of Pastoral Care

The following job description provides guidelines
which allow for flexibility in relationship to (1) the team
ministry with the pastor and staff, and (2) the priority
needs of the church.

Basic Assumption: "The function of religion at its
best is to provide a believable patterning of life from
stage to stage from birth to death for the individual
and the family in the context of the larger family of
mankind." [1] These believable patterns can be provided
in concrete terms through a (1) preventive ministry,
(2) remedial ministry, and (3) administrative ministry.

I. Preventive Ministry
   A. *Family Life Education*—The objective will
be to relate Christian teachings and values
to the areas of

(1) Premarital guidance, (2) human sexuality, (3) marital adjustments, and (4) family relationships. The family life education will be implemented through:

1. An *annual emphasis* such as a Family Life Conference.
2. *Retreats* such as Marriage Enrichment Retreats, Family Enrichment Retreats, and Christian Growth Retreats.
3. *Small groups* such as Christian Growth Groups, Family Clusters, and Special Needs Groups.
4. Integration into the *ongoing educational program* of the church in cooperation with the minister of religious education.

B. *Worship*—Participate and help in the planning of the worship services. This would include preaching at least once a month.
C. *New Members*—Will be visited as part of an orientation to the services of the church and community.

II. Remedial Ministry

A. *Counseling*—This will include: (1) personal adjustment, (2) premarital, (3) marital, (4) family, (5) vocational, and (6) group counseling. Trust is of the utmost importance in a counseling relationship. Therefore, information given in confidence will not be shared with anyone without the person's permission.
B. *The Hospital and Crises Ministry* will be shared with the pastor.

    C. *Ministry Training*—Interested persons will be trained to minister to specific needs and people.

    D. The major responsibilities of the pastor will be assumed when he is away.

III. Administrative Ministry

    A. The pastor will be supported as the leader of the church.

    B. The Preventive and Remedial Ministries will be implemented and administered.

    C. The minister of pastoral care's ministry will be integrated into the other programs of the church.

    D. The major responsibilities of the pastor will be assumed when he is away.

    E. The minister of pastoral care will "oversee" the work of the El Paso and Juarez missions.

    F. He will serve on appropriate committees and help plan the annual calendar.

Minister to Senior Adults

1. He will work with senior adults sixty years and older.

2. He will work with the Adult Division director and the volunteer workers in Adult 5, 6, and 7 in developing the program.

3. He will organize a weekday ministry which will include Bible study, fellowship, and ministry to others. This will begin with our church but extend to all interested senior adults in the community.

4. He will oversee the ministry to homebound per-

sons and those in the convalescent homes. Any relevant information about these persons will be passed on to the pastor and the "Deacons on Call."

5. He will work under the direction of the pastor and in close association with the education director. He will establish a flexible schedule to cover the above procedures.

6. His work hours will be halftime with two weeks of vacation a year.

Minister of Single Adult Education
Principal Function:

The minister of single adult education is responsible to the administrator for coordinating and promoting the student and single adult educational program.

Regular Duties:

1. Coordinate the Student/Single departments in Sunday School, Church Training, and weekday activities; recommend and implement approved promotional projects.

2. Enlist and train leadership.

3. Develop a program of fellowships, retreats, and seminars for this age group.

4. Develop goals for the work with students and singles.

5. Lead workers in systematic program of visitation.

6. Keep abreast of latest educational methods.

7. Prepare budget request for approval; maintain budget.

8. Preach and teach as assigned.

9. Perform other duties as assigned.

Note

1. Wayne E. Oates, *When Religion Gets Sick* (Philadelphia: Westminster Press, 1970), p. 83. Used by permission.

For Further Study

Henry, Mark and Mary Frances. *A Patchwork Family*. Nashville: Broadman Press, 1978.

5
Planning Family Ministry

The most effective programs are those in which the most time and energy have been invested in the planning stage. Like other phases of the church's work, family ministry will not take place if it has not been planned.

There are two aspects of all church planning—long range and annual. Both are necessary for a well-balanced program of family ministry. We will deal with annual planning and with five-year plans rather than with a longer span.

The involvement of the target group in planning is important if needs are to be met. Since family ministry involves three distinctive types of work—with families, with singles, and with senior adults—these three groups may be responsible for, or at least involved in, planning.

Advantages of involving the target group in planning are obvious. Needs and interests will not be missed. Groups are much more responsive to activities which they have helped to plan than they are to those handed down. Enlistment is easier when the program is *ours* instead of *theirs*. People feel trusted and worthwhile when their opinions are sought.

Churches work in different ways to get planning done. In some, the pastor and other staff members alone are involved in family ministry planning. Others have a family ministry planning committee. In some churches the church council is responsible, while in others the deacons will be assigned this responsibility. Long-range planning committees are sometimes charged with making general plans in all areas, including family ministry, usually for a five- to ten-year period.

Planning for the family may be done by a planning group composed of couples. Staff members (usually the pastor, assistant pastor, or minister of education if there is no family life director) will lead the planning session. If there is a family ministry committee, members of that committee will also be involved; or they may have total responsibility.

Plans will be reviewed and evaluated by the families in the church and then referred to the church council for approval and incorporation into the total church calendar.

If there is a senior adult council, that group may lead the planning for senior adults. Otherwise representatives from senior adult Sunday School classes or a committee appointed by the leader of the weekday senior adult group may assume this responsibility.

Planning for single adults may be done by the single adult council. The council may wish to make surveys of interest and felt needs. They will be responsible for planning activities to meet interests and needs of the group.

There are three approaches to planning illustrated

here. Each is illustrated by plans for one of the segments of family ministry (families, senior adult, or single adult). These illustrations are not to be interpreted to mean that one method is more appropriate for any group than it is for the others.

The Grid Approach

One approach for planning is the *grid.* It is illustrated here by showing how a program for families can be planned. Some churches will have more activities than these; some, fewer. Some may want to plan for more areas; some, less. Not every area of interest will be covered every year. A better balance can be achieved if planning covers at least a five-year period, however.

Annually, the planning grid may be reviewed and updated, with detailed plans completed. Dates, leaders, and other details will be added for each event. Promotion and publicity plans will be made and responsibility assigned.

Annual Emphasis Approach

Another approach which may be used is the annual emphasis approach, illustrated here by a senior adult plan for five years. In this approach, an annual emphasis is selected for each year. Activities related to the emphasis are blocked in; and, when time for completion of the planning arrives, other activities will be added.

For example, the completed calendar for the first year for senior adults might be something like this. (We're assuming that this group meets weekly on a weekday.)

Area of Concern	Activities for 19___	Activities for 19___	Activities for 19___	Activities for 19___	Activities for 19___
Family Communication	Family Enrichment Retreat	Study Family Enrichment books (all age groups)	Parent-Teen Dialogues	Family Enrichment Retreat	Family Enrichment Retreat Reading program involving all age groups
Marriage Enrichment	Marriage Enrichment Retreat	Two Marriage Enrichment Retreats Reading Program - **Building a Better Marriage**	Four Marriage Enrichment Retreats Bible Study on Marriage	Four Marriage Enrichment Retreats	Four Marriage Enrichment Retreats
Preparation for Marriage (planned jointly with Single Adult Council)	Engaged Couple Retreat	Teach **Made for Each Other** to young adults and older youth Engaged Couple Retreat	Two Engaged Couples Retreats Family-Marriage Study for Children	Youth Look at Marriage: Seminar	**It's OK to Be Single** taught to older youth and younger adults Two Engaged Couples Retreats
Sex Education	Parent-Youth Dialogue on Sex	Reading Program - Sex Education Series	Sex Education Workshop for Parents	Parent/Youth Dialogues on Sex	Sex Education Workshop for Parents
Family Money Management	Reading Program - Money Management	Individual counseling on money management available	Reading Program - Money Management	Money Management Conferences	Study age-group money management series
Parenting	Reading Program - **Growing Parents Growing Children**	Parenting Workshops on use of **Living with Teenagers**	Parenting Conference	Reading Program (using Parenting Bibliography)	Quarterly parent meetings, preschool, children, youth
Families Serving			Conferences: Family Serving	Conferences: Family Serving	Conferences: Family Serving

19__ Emphasis: Hobbies	19__ Emphasis: Volunteer Service	19__ Emphasis: Travel (Armchair and otherwise)	19__ Emphasis: Continuing Education	19__ Emphasis: Second Career
Classes in Macrame Ceramics Oil Painting Knitting Woodwork Creative Writing Gardening Attend local Craft Fair	Bible Study on Service Field trip to community agencies using volunteers Training for ministry (at least 5 areas of interest to group) Recognition of volunteers in worship service	Travel films at each meeting Reading and report program on places of interest Slide shows by members Quarterly short trips and one longer trip for group	Study: **Never Too Old to Learn** Field trip to local college to learn matriculation procedure Testimonies from senior adults involved in continuing education Presentation of other adult education opportunities College extension or other college-level courses offered at church building	Emphasis on one career at each monthly meeting Testimonies from those in second careers Training for new careers (offered either by church or by community)

October 3, 10, 17, and 24
Bible study—Mr. Blair
Macrame lesson—Mrs. Kent
Ceramics lesson—Mrs. Watts
November 1, 8, 15, 22
Bible study—Mrs. Helmes
Oil painting class—Mr. Burns
Macrame class—Mrs. Kent
Ceramics class—Mrs. Watts
November 29 and December 5, 12
Bible study—Mr. Gillespie
Christmas decorations workshop—Mr. and Mrs.
Lackey
December 19
Christmas party for Riverview Rest Home
December 26
Bible study—Mr. Gillespie
Oil painting class—Mr. Burns
Macrame class—Mrs. Kent
Ceramics class—Mrs. Watts
January 2, 9, 16, 23
Bible study—Mrs. Nichols
Knitting class—Mrs. Walker
Woodwork class—Mr. Bradley
Creative writing class—Miss Ayers
January 30
Houseplant clinic—Ray's Flower Shop in charge
February 6, 13, 20, 27
Bible study—Mrs. MacBeth
Getting Ready to Garden—Mr. and Mrs. Baldwin

The remainder of the year may be detailed in the same way, with hobby emphasis given a major portion of each program.

Goal-Strategy Approach

To achieve the overall objective of enriching the lives of single adults, the single adult council may select a number of goals with measurable and dated strategies covering a period of three to five years. For example:

Goal 1: We will provide counsel and help for divorced persons in our church and community.

We will achieve this goal by:

(1) Conducting _____ seminars for divorced persons each year.

(2) Seeking to enlist _____ persons in each seminar.[1]

(3) Providing a counseling service for divorced persons on a part-time basis by _____ (date) and on a full-time basis by _____ (date).

(4) Providing a monthly fellowship hour for formerly-married persons in homes or at the church.

(5) Working with the media center in providing and distributing annually a bibliography for divorced persons.

Goal 2: We will provide help for single parents in our church and community.

We will achieve this goal by:

(1) Providing, when it is needed, a program of activities for children of single parents while their parents are involved in single-parent activities, beginning _____ (date).

(2) Providing a monthly fellowship hour for single

parents in homes or at the church, beginning ____ (date).

(3) Providing annually a seminar for single parents, with agenda determined by a survey among single parents themselves.

Goal 3: We will provide service opportunities for single adults.

(1) By ____ (date) we will have surveyed our church and community to discover ways in which singles may serve, and will have surveyed singles to determine which opportunities are of interest to them.

(2) By ____ (date) we will have at least ____ projects (such as painting the building used by a mission, sponsoring a softball team in the ghetto, taking orphanage children on outings) under way with a minimum of ____ singles involved.

(3) By ____ (date) we will have involved at least ____ percent of singles in at least one service opportunity; by ____ (date) we will have involved at least ____ percent.[1]

(4) By ____ we will have sponsored a mission service project with singles, at their own expense, for one to two weeks in cooperation with the Home and/or Foreign Mission Board.

Goal 4: We will counteract loneliness by providing fellowship opportunities for singles.

(1) By ____ we will have started a weekly activity time for singles with a wide range of recreational and fellowship activities.

(2) By ____ we will have reached ____ percent of the singles in the church in this weekly fellowship program.[1]

(3) By _____ (date) this fellowship program will be enlarged to at least five nights a week.

(4) By _____ (date) our church will have rented or purchased a single adult center for all single adult activities.

Goal 5: We will provide growth opportunities involving a minimum of _____ percent of all singles in the church in activities other than the church program organizations.[1]

(1) By _____ (date) we will have had one retreat, one seminar, and one workshop on topics selected by the singles.

(2) By _____ (date) we will have offered at least one seminar, retreat, or workshop each quarter.

(3) By _____ (date) we will have ongoing seminars and workshops meeting weekly.

Goal 6: We will provide assistance to members of the church who lose spouses by death.

(1) We will conduct a grief seminar by _____ (date).

(2) By _____ we will have set up a program for contacts by widowed in our group in the homes of the surviving spouse when there is a death in our church fellowship.

After singles have reviewed plans for evaluation and suggestions for changes and additions have been made, plans will go to the church council for approval and correlation with the total church program. The single adult council will then begin work on detailing the plans. Suppose, for example, that the plans call for a seminar to be given within a specified year. The single adult council will set a date after studying the church calendar and other events that might affect singles. Seminar leaders will be selected and enlisted. Finances will be planned. Will a fee be charged? If not, are funds available from the church budget? Publicity committees will be selected and enlisted. If single parents are involved, plans will need to be made for their children. If subcommittees (publicity, children's program, room arrangement, refreshments, or others) are needed, regular check-up and progress reporting may be scheduled.

An evaluation committee may also be needed. Feedback from the group attending this seminar will be of great help in planning the next one.

An annual single adult calendar may be printed. Churchwide activities involving singles and all activities planned for singles will be entered on the calendar. Copies may be made available to members and prospects.

Sample Calendar

OCTOBER

Pre-Sunday School Coffee Fellowships

October 6—Single Adult I in charge

October 13—Single Adult I in charge

October 20—Thirty-niners in charge

October 27—College Singles in charge

Single Parent Fellowship: October 26

Ghostly Gala: October 31

All singles and children from Baptist Orphanage—

Stewart's farm

Wednesday night seminar: Building Self-esteem

October 2—You're Somebody!—Dr. Baker

October 9—Being Authentic—Mrs. Williams

October 16—Decision Making—Dr. Baker

October 23—Humility *vs.* Pride—Dr. Allen

October 30—Expectations: Reality or Fantasy—Mrs. Williams

NOVEMBER

State Singles' Retreat, Seaview State Park, November 2–4

Wednesday Afternoon Hobby Seminars
November 7, 14, 21, 28

Class guitar—Tony Phillips

Drama—Becky Thompson

Needlepoint—Sarah Gibbons

Leadership Training—Dr. Owens

Chess—Ralph Bowen

Christmas Decorations—Bob Wright and Joan French

A Night on Broadway Show—November 17
(Presentation by the drama workshop)

Cooperative Thanksgiving Dinner—church
5:30 Thanksgiving Day

DECEMBER

Caroling

December 6—Sunny View Nursing Home

December 13—Golden Age Retirement Center

December 20—El Centro Mall

December 23—Riverview Mall

December 24—Baptist Hospital

Cooperative Christmas Dinner, church, 5:30
Christmas Day

New Year's Eve Party—December 31

8:00 Dinner at Central Hotel

9:30 Game party at church

11:00 Worship and dedication service

The annual program for senior adults or families may also be planned by use of goals and strategies.

Whether you use any of these approaches or a combination of all, planning is essential if you want to make your program for singles, seniors, and families the best that it can be. Whatever you want, plan for it!

Evaluation

The planning cycle involves evaluation. After a project is completed, evaluation provides feedback into the next cycle of planning (and sometimes into the next project).

Plan→Conduct→Evaluate→Plan→Conduct→Evaluate

Sophisticated testing is usually not practical for churches, but simple questionnaires may be used. Usually these will be unsigned; responses will be more honest if anonymity is preserved. In many instances older persons have a tendency to give the "polite" response rather than adverse criticism, but this is not always true.

The following is an example of an evaluation form.

Conference Evaluation

The objective of this conference was *to help parents and youth grow in their ability to communicate with one another.*

Do you feel that objective relates to needs in your family?

—— Yes   —— No   —— Somewhat

How well do you feel that objective was achieved in your family?

—— Very well —— Not at all —— Somewhat

Which part was most helpful? _____

In what way could the conference have met your needs in a better way? _____

_____

_____

_____

What would you suggest as objectives of future parent-youth conferences?

Are you:

_____ Father

_____ Mother

_____ Youth, male

_____ Youth, female

Tabulate the information, with cross tabulation by categories. For example, your summary of responses to the above questionnaire might look like this:

	Men	Women	Boys	Girls
Total number responses	20	24	22	39
Felt objective related to needs	3(15%)	17(70%)	9(41%)	3(7%)
Felt objective did not relate to needs	12(60%)	4(16%)	9(41%)	3(7%)
Felt objective somewhat related to needs	5(25%)	3(12%)	7(31%)	12(30%)

Felt objective achieved very well	8(41%)	10(42%)	3(14%)	5(13%)
Felt objective achieved not at all	3(15%)	2(8%)	12(54%)	19(48%)
Felt objective somewhat achieved	9(45%)	12(50%)	12(32%)	15(39%)

Conclusion

Men and boys were not as aware of communication needs as were women and girls.

Youth did not receive as much help from the conference as did their parents.

Implications

Men and boys may need help in recognizing communication gaps and/or need for communication. A father-son conference may be needed.

More involvement of youth is needed in planning process for next project to help discover ways to meet their needs.

Tabulation of results is important because it helps leaders look at information objectively. It helps avoid their seeing only the things they want to see, and it helps identify problem areas. The time used in tabulation is well spent.

Putting It Over

The program has been planned. Activities have been scheduled. Now what? How do we get people there?

First of all, get the best person or persons available

as project leaders. Let the leader know exactly the purpose of the meeting, the amount of time, the setting, and something about the interests, needs, and background of the participants.

Then let all of those for whom the meeting is planned know the details. One announcement from the pulpit will not be enough. Through the church mail-out, if there is such, and perhaps through the local newspapers and radio, through posters, and by telephone and word of mouth, share the word. Direct mail may be effective if it is well done.

Avoid "you should" and "you ought to" invitations. Family ministry projects are planned to help people where they hurt and to help them solve and/or prevent problems. If people have a need and if they recognize that an activity will help to meet that need, they will come.

Satisfied customers—those who have participated in similar activities in the past—are the best persons to serve on the enlistment committee. A senior adult who has been on a retreat and benefited from the experience can influence others to participate in future retreats. Couples who have been blessed through a marriage enrichment retreat will invite their friends to the next retreat—whether they're on the enlistment committee or not. A testimony time in the appropriate group will encourage others to attend. In an adult Sunday School department period, or even in a worship service, a couple may be asked to share their feelings about a project in which they participated.

Family ministry programs dreamed up on Wednesday afternoon and conducted the following Sunday may be better than no family ministry—or they may not. But in order to enrich the lives of families in the church, planning is essential.

Note

1. Weekday single adult activities are *want-to* rather than *ought-to* programs. Efforts will be directed toward providing programs to meet interests and needs of singles and to making them aware of opportunities, not to coercing them to participate. Attendance goals are not to be used to promote attendance.

For Further Study

Knight, George. *Ministering to Families: a Planning Guide*. Nashville: Convention Press, 1971.

McDonough, Reginald M. *Leading Your Church in Long-Range Planning*. Nashville: Convention Press, 1975.

6
Projects and Activities

Most churches do not have an ongoing organization for family ministry, but carry out this work through specially planned projects. A project may be defined as an activity that has a definite beginning and end: it is not ongoing. Although not a comprehensive list, this chapter will identify some projects and activities that may be used by churches.

Four types of formats are often used:

• *Conference*—lecture-oriented, with presentations; leader-centered, with conferees listening as participants in the process.

• *Retreats*—Modular in design and restricted in membership, this format is more experiential and is usually located in a place apart.

• *Course* or *seminar*—presentation and discussion, led by resource persons of specialized expertise.

• *Workshop*—task-group oriented, with participants involved in assigned tasks and the people themselves being the resource persons.

A project may frequently be a combination of two or more of these formats, named by the predominant characteristics.

The following projects are presently in frequent use by church groups:

Marriage Enrichment Retreats

Since the first formal marriage enrichment retreats in 1961, hundreds of thousands of couples have attended seminars, retreats, and conferences for the purpose of enhancing their marriages. These are not couples whose marriages are in trouble. Most of these are couples who believe they have good marriages and want to make them better. And they see such events as practical and effective ways to improve communications, acquire more skills in conflict resolution and life-planning, and open up access for greater intimacy in marriage.

There are organizations now dedicated to the enrichment of marriages. Among these are the Association of Couples for Marriage Enrichment, founded by David and Vera Mace, and Marriage Encounter, originating with Father Calvo, of Spain, and the Catholic Christian Family Movement.

The Family Ministry Department of the Baptist Sunday School Board is building a National Marriage Enrichment System, with carefully planned and supervised retreat models on three levels. The Basic Marriage Enrichment Retreat has been published in kit form for those leader couples who train in its use. A further development of intermediate and advanced level models is planned for the near future. These models all require couples to go to a retreat site for two days to participate, under trained leadership, in activities designed for experiential growth in marital relationships.

Parent Enrichment Workshops

Parent-child relationships are the focus of a growing number of programs for the enhancement of parenthood. Two of these programs are Parent Effectiveness Training, originated by Thomas Gordon (author of the book by that name), requiring trained leadership, and Systematic Training for Effective Parenting, by Don Dinkmeyer and Gary McKay, designed to be self-taught.

Most parent enrichment programs work with the parents in the areas of understanding themselves and their task, understanding their children, and teaching communication and problem-solving skills. These programs usually take a seminar or workshop format in a series of weekly sessions with homework assignments. Some programs contain graded sessions targeting parents of children in specific ages (parents of preschoolers, parents of elementary-age children, and parents of teenagers).

The Family Ministry Department of the Baptist Sunday School Board conducts workshops and leadership training for Parent Enrichment Workshops and has published a full-length reference for parents. This practical guidebook for Christian parents and a resource for workshops in a local church is entitled *Growing Parents Growing Children,* by Dr. W. Wayne Grant, pediatrician.

Family Enrichment Conferences

The purpose of a Family Enrichment Conference is to provide an environment where information can be received, where new insights and deeper feelings can be developed, and where positive action can be taken to enrich the quality of family living. Individual growth and greater harmony in family relationships should result from a Family Enrichment Conference.

A Family Enrichment Conference conducted during Christian Home Week and at other times of the year is one way in which areas of need not included in other places in the church's curriculum can be given attention. Some subjects that have been only partially covered in other discussions in the church may be developed in more detail through a Family Enrichment Conference.

The Family Enrichment Conference should not be regarded as a clinic for sick families or a therapy group for deteriorated family relationships. Rather, it is a way of making healthy families more competent and enhancing the good relationships that already exist. Couples who have a good marriage but want to make it better should be encouraged to attend the Family Enrichment Conference so that they can provide insights for other persons seeking them. Each family has its own strengths as well as its weaknesses.

Hopefully, the environment in the Family Enrichment Conference will be so supportive and accepting that each participant can be honest in discussion periods. However, it should also be so informative that new insights can be gained and needs can be clearly recognized. The Family Enrichment Conference should create a desire for growth and change. It should enable the participants to gain some skills in bringing about these changes for positive good. Change calls for adjustments, and thus families begin using the problem-solving techniques developed in the Family Enrichment Conference.

Good marriages and family relationships do not just happen. They are brought about by hard work and total commitment. And the church needs to do everything possible to see that family enrichment is a reality in the lives of its church members. Sample programs for family enrichment conferences are found in the Appendix, along with a list of Family Enrichment Series books published by The Sunday School Board of the Southern Baptist Convention.

Family Enrichment Retreats

Like the Family Enrichment Conference, the Family Enrichment Retreat is for the whole family and serves the same purposes. The retreat format, however, involves more experiential learning and leisure activities, with intergenerational designs predominant in the agenda. Held in a place apart, where family recreational facilities are available, the Family Enrichment Retreat seeks to enable family members to participate *together* in experiences that enhance them as a family. These retreats are designed to do for family relationships what marriage enrichment retreats do for marriage relationships. The Family Ministry Department of the Baptist Sunday School Board has developed a model for this type of event.

Parenting workshops or conferences deal with problems of parenting. Usually set up according to the age of children (preschool, elementary, junior high, or senior high), they identify and propose solutions to problems parents face. Such books as *Growing Parents Growing Children* by Wayne Grant may be used as basic resources. Problems and possible solutions come from the group in their study together or from resource persons if the conference format is used.

The purpose of a *Parent-Teen Dialogue* is to help parents and teens better understand and trust one another. We fear the unknown. We certainly don't trust what we don't understand.

Parent-teen dialogues also help each group recognize the benefits of interchange with the other and lead them to actually begin to do it.

A PTD (Parent-Teen Dialogue) is an experience the church plans to encourage parents and teenagers to talk together. It can last for a single session, an afternoon, much of a day, or a longer time, such as a retreat. The church schedules the meeting, encourages attendance, and plans the activities that will help bring about the desired result.

The meeting usually starts with the youth in one group and the parents in another. This is much less threatening. Each group will be involved in activities that will help them better understand one another.

For example, the adults could list things that remind them of how they felt as teenagers or of how different life today is from their lives then. Youth might share in a Bible study about parental responsibilities or explore what is involved in family finance. Each generation needs to begin to see things from the perspective of the other.

Then both groups will get together. Use nonfamily groupings at first—two adults and three youth, none of them related. The youth need to outnumber the adults. They will tend to be reserved anyway, especially if they feel ganged up on.

These temporary "families" will get acquainted and then report to each other on what they discovered when they were apart. Next they may jot down such things as their favorite food; ways they relax; music, movies, and TV shows they like; people they admire; things that concern them. Each person will share each response in turn and tell *why* he responded as he did. Notice that they will gradually be sharing more vital things. A similar sharing in actual family groups may be the next part of the agenda.

Deemphasize lecture and stress involvement in PTD. Instead of planning talks, plan talking. Plan actual dialogue. Plan interchange.

Preparation for marriage seminars (sometimes called engaged couples retreats) is designed to help engaged couples consider realistically the marriage experience. Large churches may schedule these seminars quarterly; smaller churches may cooperate with other churches in the city, area, or state in providing these projects. Books such as *Letters to Karen* and *Letters to Philip* by Shedd may be used. Films such as *Marriage, What Kind for You?* and the test "Taylor-Johnson Temperament Analysis Profile" may also be included. A bibliography on marriage and the family will be useful.

Divorce seminars are becoming increasingly popular with the growing divorce rate. Some churches have had fantastic response to the divorce seminars. Those recently divorced (or sometimes those contemplating divorce) are invited to participate. Each group may build its own program based on needs, or such books as *An Open Book to the Christian Divorcee* by Roger Crook may be studied.

Seminar participants indicate that one of the most helpful aspects is competent leaders who have personally experienced divorce. They need not be divorced persons in order to be effective, but they must possess understanding and empathy for the divorced persons. Persons who have been close to divorce are more likely to have understanding and empathy.

Grief seminars are planned as support for widowed persons. Studies of such resources as *Good Grief* by Westberg, *A Grief Observed* by Lewis, or *Joy Beyond Grief* by Anderson help the widowed to learn to work through their grief. These should be short-term projects. There is a danger that the seminar might become a crutch that deters healing if it is carried on too long. Grief seminars may be sponsored by a group of churches rather than by a single church; but larger churches, especially those with many older members, may conduct their own. Persons who have participated in grief seminars may become resource persons for individual ministry to others in the membership who suffer loss.

Sex education workshops meet a need in many churches. Some church leaders feel very strongly that sex education for children and youth should not be conducted by schools or churches, but that it is the responsibility of the homes. Others feel that churches can assist the home and meet a need by providing sex education from the perspective of Christian teachings and values.

Sex education workshops or conferences for parents to receive training in teaching their children about human sexuality are beneficial. Parents are then able to assume responsibility for providing sex education for their own children. Those parents welcome an opportunity to work with other parents in planning ways to meet the needs of their children more effectively.

Many parents are fearful of sex education in schools because moral and religious values are not emphasized, and they would like to learn at home how to teach these values to their children at home.

Such books as the following may be used in sex education workshop for parents:

Made to Grow, Harty

The Changing Me, Edens

Growing Up with Sex, Crawford and Simmons

Sex Is More Than a Word, Lester

Made for Each Other, Drakeford

Teaching Your Children About Sex, Howell

If churches wish to conduct classes for children and youth, appropriate books from the above list may be used.

Money management conferences are needed in most churches. Marriage counselors indicate that finances are a major source of family problems. The entire family can be involved in studying such books as the following:

$taying in the Black Financially, Bloskas (adults)

$: a Handbook on Money for Youth, Williamson (senior high youth)

Dad, About My Allowance . . . , Clark (junior high youth)

If I Had a Money Tree, Fulbright (middle school children)

My Family's Money, Caldwell (younger school children).

Other publishers also have resources for conferences of this nature.

Reading programs are another kind of project churches may find effective. With the increasing popularity of church libraries or media centers, suitable resources are available to more and more church members.

Bibliographies on any subject of family concern may be made available to church members. Books may be displayed in the church library and members encouraged to read in areas of their needs and interests. Some type of recognition may be given for a completion of a specified number of books. Discussion groups may be an outgrowth of reading programs.

Enrichment for single adults may include seminars, conferences, workshops, or retreats. Personal and spiritual growth is primary, but fellowship also is an important aspect. Content may include such practical matters as hobbies, cooking for one, budgeting for a single-parent family, appliance repair, or planning a vacation. Other topics included might be improving self-concept, growing spiritually, developing a Christian life-style, or making new friends. Singles themselves should have major responsibility in planning and conducting these projects, enlisting as leaders persons with expertise in areas of concern. These will usually be weekday activities.

Enrichment for senior adults may use the seminar, conference, workshop, or retreat format. Personal and spiritual enrichment as well as fellowship are important aspects of senior adult projects. Program suggestions for weekday groups are found in *Mature Living,* a monthly magazine published by The Sunday School Board of the Southern Baptist Convention. These suggestions may be used for projects if there is no ongoing weekday group.

Family clusters may also be considered as a project,

although they may exist for a longer period of time than most other projects. This is a relatively new concept which has come into being because of the need for an extended family. Many families in our mobile society are far from relatives, and the clustering program groups families (including single parents, other singles, and senior adults) for Bible study, fellowship, worship, and ministry.

Clusters may get together as often as they wish and for the type of activities they wish to engage in. They become the "family" to help in times of need. (See pp. 51–52.)

Christian Home Week—Many churches observe Christian Home Week, suggested for the week preceding Mother's Day. Sermons on the Christian home, along with seminars on study groups, are often features of this week. Southern Baptists provide age-graded books for study during this week. A sample program for Christian Home Week and a list of the Family Enrichment Series books are included in the appendix.

Family recreation—In cooperation with church recreation leaders, family recreation activities may be scheduled. Camping trips, bicycle trips, hikes, family nights in activities buildings, and other types of activities will help draw family members closer together.

Family life education—Along with other education offered by the church, education for family life and marriage must be considered. As special studies or as a part of the regular curriculum of ongoing organizations, churches may offer to preschoolers, youth, and adults education in family living.

With changing life-styles and emphasis on the single life, churches may help persons become aware that marriage and the family are not the only options open to them. Along with positive teachings about marriage, there may be positive teachings about singleness. Learning from childhood that singlehood is a choice will help persons who choose the single life to avoid feelings of guilt.

Equipping centers are the result of a new concept which may be used for education in family life. Short-term projects, usually using the small-group approach, may be scheduled to study any area of family life. Resources are available from the Church Training Department of The Sunday School Board of the Southern Baptist Convention and from other denominational publishing houses. These studies may be scheduled on Sunday evenings, Saturday mornings, or any evening during the week.

Do-it-yourself models—Church leaders with extensive training in family ministry may be interested in designing their own projects. Richard Waggener has adapted material prepared originally by Freida Gardner, providing suggestions for designing and implementing models. The sections on administration and recruitment/promotion are applicable for use with any model.

Outline of Process for Designing Educational Models in the Local Church

I. *Determine target/focus group.* This is a person-centered approach that calls for the planners' attention to be focused first upon the persons to be ministered to.

  A. Key questions about the target group:

    1. For whom? Who needs help? Family

status, age(s), location in personal development? Where are these people in their personal pilgrimage in life?

2. How broad a spectrum of needs will be the focus? Who can profit most from this event, and who will profit least?

3. What is already being done to meet these needs, and how does this event fit into that?

4. What can be done to enhance or extend what is already being done?

5. What does the target group itself seem to want? To what will they respond? What is their point of felt need?

B. Ways of studying the target group or determining the target group:

1. Use opinionnaire or questionnaire.

2. Ask other professionals, peers, mental health personnel, family physicians, teachers who are in the business of helping families.

3. Personal interview with possible focus persons.

4. Self-reflection. Trust your insights.

5. Series of minisessions wherein discussion is encouraged. Often people have not formulated clear thinking about their needs, and open sessions that are part instructive and part dialogue will prompt new thinking wherein the people can better define needs and wants.

6. Provide elective courses and see which ones gain voluntary response.

II. *Define objectives.* What do we expect to accomplish? (These can be both instructional and behavioral objectives.)
   A. Definitions:
      1. An *objective* is a *statement of purpose* that is *comprehensive* enough to include all that you expect to do *and specific* enough to clearly define the definition you plan to take in accomplishing your purpose.
      2. A *goal* is a statement of dated intent embodying a measurable quantity and/or quality of results (for example, "Our goal is to have three hundred families regularly subscribing to *Home Life* magazine by January 1, 1979").
   Note: In planning a family life education model, there may be no need for stating a goal by the definition given it above. This is relevant to planning a family ministry program encompassing a lengthy period.
   B. Four elements in educational models by which to test an objective:
      1. *Knowledge* or understanding gains involving facts, concepts, theories, and inquiries.
      2. *Skills* acquisition involving the how-to instruction and experience in practice.
      3. *Attitudes* assessment involving feelings, life positions, identity of self and others.
      4. *Values* clarification involving principle and priority.
   Note: The more of these elements which are

incorporated into the objective of the model, the more *wholistic* is the learning that takes place.

C. Key questions in writing objectives:

1. Do you expect the same level of achievement from everyone? How realistic is the expectation you have in this statement?

2. How will you and the target group members both know you have what you started out to get?

3. Can you quote your objective from memory? Have you so lived with it and processed it that you know it, word for word?

D. Awareness of "mushy" words and definitive words. *Some words open to interpretations:*

"to understand"

"to appreciate"

"to grasp the significance of"

"to believe, have faith in"

"to have an awareness of"

Words open to fewer interpretations:

"to identify"

"to solve"

"to experience"

"to differentiate"

"to use one's ability to"

"to demonstrate"

"to enumerate"

III. *Select format.* What grouping approach best facilitates the objective and its target?

A. Key questions to be considered:

1. What size group (or groups) do you expect to serve at one time?
2. What readiness is manifest in the target group for the level of learning projected?
3. Will the design be freestanding, or will it be an integral part of another curriculum?

IV. *Decide location and timing.*

A. Key questions:
   1. How intense or personal is the learning experience being projected?
   2. How will interruptions affect the learning experience?
   3. What events must not be in competition with the event(s) planned?
   4. What effect will the location and the timing have upon the meaning or feeling atmosphere of the event?
   5. What cost is feasible?

B. Possible locations:
   1. Church building, sanctuary, educational or recreational space.
   2. Home(s).
   3. Public facilities (school, community center, university center).
   4. Conference center.
   5. Resort, retreat area, encampment.

C. Possible timing:
   1. Consecutive schedule.
      a. Weekend, including Sunday.
      b. Weekend, excluding Sunday.
      c. Sunday through Wednesday.

         d.   Weeknight series.

     2. Intermittent schedule

         a. Sunday School series.

         b. Wednesday evening series.

         c. Other weekly series.

V. *Plan content: teaching-learning activities.*

    A. Key considerations:

       1. Appropriateness of learning activities . . .

         . . . to subject matter

         . . . to constituents

         . . . to the objectives

         . . . to the institution sponsoring the event.

       2. Timing-Pacing to the capacity of constituents.

       3. Teacher/Facilitator competency.

       4. Acceptance level of the constituents.

       5. Cost (films, outside resource persons, luxury of surroundings).

       6. Equipment available.

       7. Variety (appeal to all senses; relieve boredom).

       8. Developmental appropriateness.

       9. Sequence of learning: What will come next?

    B. Some possible teaching-learning activities:

lecture	brainstorming
audiovisuals	buzz groups
(including videotape)	directed reading
circular response	discussion
colloquy	field trip
paired reading review	resource person

panel	symposium
role play	drama/skits
visual aids	games
simulation	values
structured experience	clarification
demonstration	fishbowl

VI. *Discover and enlist resources.*

A. People resources:

Search the community for people with special interests and/or skills in the area of your ministry and enlist them well in advance of the dates of events. Guidance counselors in public-school systems, case workers in mental-health centers, physicians, psychologists, chaplains, teachers (with special skills), employment counselor, personnel officers, university professors, ministers (with special skills). Sometimes housewives have left some of these jobs to devote full-time to homemaking career and would welcome the opportunity to contribute again out of professional skills. Ask around.

B. Other resources:

Mental-health associations, the Planned Parenthood Association, and other community help organizations have book and audiovisual libraries available to the public. Home demonstration units of public utility companies and community extension services provide package services in family life education.

VII. *Set up administration.*

1. Coordinate with other programs.

    2. Reserve the facilities.

    3. Plan the finances; budget in sponsoring institution; arrange for possible scholarships if a fee is charged.

    4. Gather the equipment.

    5. Enumerate housekeeping details, breaks, locations of conveniences, cleanup; return borrowed equipment.

    6. Leadership training, team preparation.

    7. In-house management: registration, equipment operation, errand running, hospitality functions, counseling.

    8. Evaluation structure (during and after the event).

    9. Recycling the program (use of PERT chart for long-range plans, preservation of notes, tapes, work sheets for reuse).

VIII. *Lay out recruitment/promotion approach(es).*

    A. Where are *you* with this? A positive expectation, an excitement that is natural, a *sold attitude* are essential for those who would promote this event: "Look what we've got!"

    B. Plan notice carefully. Select key words that "hook" the natural interest of people, yet do not scare them: *enrich, learn, rekindle, how to, skills, become, discover.* Envision the hearer/reader who gets the message for the first time. You understand what's happening, but will he? Invite; don't command.

    C. Give notice variously.

        1. By word printed. No form letters. Restrict general notices to main facts and ideas. No verbosity.

2. By word spoken. Public and/or private communications by word of mouth.

D. Involvement-recruitment.
   1. In the planning stages, involve key people you hope to reach. It becomes a shared responsibility, "our thing." Excitement mounts when there is personal investment.
   2. Involve those who have signed up to draw in others. Do not put pressure on people to promote until *they* are signed up themselves.

E. Timing notice. Soon enough for people to make arrangements, yet late enough to build momentum and keep it. People lose interest when they must wait too long.

IX. *Plan for evaluation and follow-up.* Design an evaluation sheet that is simple, with objective questions. Multiple-choice or evaluation continuums are good. Place in the calendar any follow-up meetings (or series) that might be appropriate for reflection upon the event months later. These help consolidate gains.

7
The Pastor and Family Ministry

The work of pastors in today's churches is seen in three categories: leadership, proclamation, and pastoral care. Ministering to families is involved in all three.

The key person in a church's ministry to families is the pastor. If he is not in support of it, family ministry will likely not be done. This is not to say that he must do it all. However, if his concern for families leads him to make family ministry a high-priority item in his own ministry, he can usually lead the church to accept the priority.

Leading the Church to Minister to Families

In the minister's leadership role, the needs of families can be kept in mind. Especially in scheduling, churches may seem to work against the family. This situation exists especially in churches having age-group programs. Extensive programs are planned for each age group, and the family is fragmented. Pressure is sometimes placed on persons to participate in every activity provided for their age group. The church may have an every-night program for all members of the family, leaving them together only in worship services—and sometimes not even then. Children's worship, youth prayer meetings, and other activities often separate the family even in traditional family periods.

Church leaders can prevent the problem by providing more intergenerational activities (activities involving all age groups) and by coordinating schedules. Family night—with many weekday activities scheduled at that time—is a partial solution. Training in ways families can use their time together may also help. Some families have no idea what to do if they find themselves together for an evening.

Ministers may use their leadership roles as means of discovering family needs. In enlisting workers, in training workers, in observation of work, and through studies of attendance records, the minister may pick up clues to problems affecting family life.

One significant contribution to family ministry which the minister can make is his own modeling of family relationships. Does he put everything else before his family? Does he feel compelled to supervise the committee cleaning the church kitchen Saturday afternoon, or can he take his son fishing? Is his wife the most neglected woman in the church?

One minister said that as he and his wife recently drove to a convention, they discovered that they didn't have much to say to each other. Neither could remember when they had taken a trip alone before; usually they had a busload of youth or senior adults or some other group for which they were responsible. They recognized on this trip that they needed to change their priorities and allow more time for each other.

The pastor can set an example by providing leadership in wholesome family living if he sees himself as a husband and father as well as a minister.

Jerry Brown, consultant in pastoral ministries, The Sunday School Board of the Southern Baptist Convention, suggests that pastors sometimes equate their relationship with God with their ministry to the church. Brown calls this idolatry. The pastor's first priority is his relationship to God; the second is his family; and the third is his church. When the pastor recognizes that his responsibility to God and his responsibility to the church are not equated, he is freed to change his values. His wife and children may receive some long-needed attention. The surprising thing is that his ministry is not hampered; it may be helped.

The pastor may also share his own pilgrimage of what being a Christian family means in his own experience. If he can accept the fact that he is human, that his family is human, and that the church does not (or should not) expect perfection from them, he may find family living more enjoyable. The goal of the pastor's family is to model normal Christianity instead of ideal Christianity.

The pastor who is human with his congregation will be more effective in his ministry. If he can let the congregation know that he has problems and difficulties as well as victories and joys, that he is struggling in his own Christian pilgrimage, he will establish a better basis for his ministry. The minister who must have the final word will lose much of his effectiveness in ministering to families.

The pastor may also lead the church to see itself as a family and to accept this role in forming relationships. *Koinonia* in the church means a family kind of dynamics in terms of support, guidance, discipline, and love.

Proclaiming Biblical Understandings of Family Life

The pastor's preaching and teaching roles give him another significant opportunity for family ministry. Many collections of sermons include family emphases. Help is available in planning preaching related to the family if the pastor feels the need of such help. For example, *Award Winning Sermons,* Volume 1, published by Broadman Press in 1977, has a section on the family.

In 1975 Dr. John Claypool preached in the Broadway Baptist Church of Fort Worth a series of four sermons on the life cycle: "The Saga of Life: Childhood"; "The Saga of Life: Adolescence"; "The Saga of Life: Adulthood"; and "The Saga of Life: Senior Adulthood." Tapes of these sermons are available from the Southern Baptist Radio and Television Commission. Dr. Claypool described this series as "a roadmap from womb to tomb."

Christian Home Week, Mother's Day, and Father's Day sermons usually center around the family. However, illustrations relating to the family may be used with sermons on many subjects.

The pastor may seek to communicate through his proclamation the love of the Father as an example for parental love. A preacher whose messages are largely criticism and condemnation often discourages members of the congregation from coming to him for further help. The church must be seen as a congregation of forgiven sinners—not one of sinless persons condemning those who sin. Needs of the congregation must be central in the pastor's sermons, along with the worth of the individual and Jesus' spirit of acceptance and redeeming love.

Giving Care to Families

In his pastoral care role, the pastor has many opportunities to serve families. Through casual contacts he often becomes aware of areas where persons are hurting. As he visits the sick, he may find that the load of guilt and sin or the heartbreak of broken relationships may be more serious than physical symptoms. Through his words of encouragement and love and affirmation, the pastor may be as effective as the physician in bringing healing.

The pastor has an opportunity for ministry in relation to weddings. Some pastors require a series of counseling sessions for all couples they marry. Others prefer to provide an engaged couples retreat once or twice a year. Then the pastor also offers young couples group sessions dealing with problems of adjustment during the first years of marriage. However he wishes to do it, preparation for marriage is a vital part of family ministry. He may want to work through the single adult council in providing premarital seminars and retreats.

One of the pastor's significant opportunities for pastoral care comes at the time of death in a church family. He may have opportunity to make suggestions regarding the funeral services. He will have opportunity to help the bereaved work through their grief in a wholesome and Christian manner.

Counseling is an important part of pastoral ministry. If a pastor has not had special training in this area, he may want to enroll in counseling training in a nearby seminary or other graduate school; or he may enter clinical training or begin a reading program in the area.

The effectiveness of the pastor's counseling will be determined by his attitudes. To summarize briefly some counseling attitudes, we would say first of all that a nonjudgmental approach is essential. If a person comes to the pastor confessing a sin in his life, an attitude of shock, condemnation, or criticism will drive the person away. Jesus' response to the woman taken in adultery serves as a model for the counselor: " 'Well then,' Jesus said, 'I do not condemn you either. Go, but do not sin again' " (John 8:11, TEV).

The pastor must believe in people and their ability to find solutions to their problems. He sees his role as that of helping them clarify their problems, not of simply providing quick and easy solutions. He must be a good listener. He may be inclined to jump ahead of the story and come up with pat answers before the counselee has finished talking. He may want to tell the counselee how to solve his problems, when sometimes listening is all that is needed.

The counselor will be conscious of people as *persons* rather than as *prospects* or *deacons* or *Sunday School teachers*. When the pastor is counseling a family in regard to the needs of their teenager who has been in trouble and he sees that the youth has been neglected, the pastor may experience personal tension. The problem may be that the parents have so many church jobs that there is no time left for the family. Can the pastor see beyond the church organizations if parents need to give up some church responsibilities? It is difficult not to be manipulative in dealing with persons when we think of the church organizations and programs instead of the individual's needs.

The same problems may arise in marital counseling. One marital partner may be neglecting the other, seemingly because of organizational responsibility in the church. The counselor, in seeking to lead the couple to discover the more basic problems, may risk losing the director of women's work or the chairman of deacons. The counselor will put the needs of the persons first.

The counselor must also be a person who can be trusted with a confidence. When a member comes to his pastor with a problem, he does not want the next Sunday's sermon to begin with, "A man I was counseling with last week told me. . . ." If the pastor uses the story at any time, it should be with permission of the person involved. Information revealed in counseling is not to be shared with anyone without the counselee's permission. If the pastor feels the need of talking the matter over with someone else, he will ask permission from the counselee before going to a doctor, attorney, or even to any other member of the church staff. Even then, anonymity will be preserved if possible; if not, confidentiality should be assured.

Empathy is essential in effective counseling. Although the problem seems trivial to the counselor, he must recognize that it is not trivial to the counselee. The counselor must be able to feel the other person's pain. He will not, however, say "I know just how you feel" because no one fully knows how another person feels. "I know you hurt and I care" is a comforting attitude.

Often the counselor will discover that the problem is not what the counselee thinks it is. More basic problems may be revealed by questions on the part of the counselor. The wife may think that her husband's drinking is the problem; the pastor may be able to see that her dependence on her father and her husband's lack of self-esteem are responsible for the drinking. The counselor must learn to look for sources behind the symptoms.

Often ministers encounter problems that demand more expertise than they have. Sometimes another person on the church staff is better prepared to handle a particular problem. Sometimes the counselor may need to refer the counselee to a Christian psychologist or psychiatrist, a mental-health center, or a physician. In referrals, he will want to make it clear that he is not dropping the counselee. "I'm with you and for you, but let's get some specialized help" will assure the counselee that he is not being rejected.

How much initiative should the pastor take in dealing with problems of members of the congregation? We asked several ministers this question: "If the pastor or other staff member is aware that a church family is having marital problems, does he offer to help or initiate counseling; or does he wait until he is asked for help?" We got these replies:

"We wait until we are asked. Help offered before it is sought is most often rejected."

"The pastor does both, depending on the people involved and the situation."

"In most cases I wait until I am asked for help. On occasion I have called the husband and asked him for lunch. In this case, I talk about the part he is willing to discuss and offer help for the future."

"Sometimes one, sometimes the other, depending on the individual case and the nature of the problem.

This can be delicate and difficult. It might also depend on how many and who are being involved with said person(s) and problem(s)."

"We often initiate. I feel free, as does the pastor, to call people when I hear there is a crisis and ask to come for a visit. I have had only one rejection in nearly four years."

"I consider it my calling before God to take the initiative and ask members how they are doing and if anything is going on. I pay careful attention to the common transitions in life that initiate crises: birth, conversion, vocational change, illness, death, divorce, separation, new responsibilities, retirement, parenting stress, isolation, withdrawal, changes in behavior and patterns of church involvement, exchanges in committee and other meetings."

One pastor made this suggestion: "Relate to persons on a daily contact basis to avoid 'crisis orientation' contact. A telephone call, a quick note, and regular visits in homes prepare an atmosphere of trust and companionship that is essential to effective ministry in troubled times."

The general feeling seems to be that the counselor can offer help but that he cannot force it on persons. He can let the family know that he is concerned and available; they must take the next step.

Families can be the organizing principle of the minister's work. Family care is not a hindrance to the *real* work of the ministry; family care *is* the ministry.

Note

1. Ernest Mosley, *Called to Joy* (Nashville: Convention Press, 1973).

For Further Study

Books

Bryant, Marcus, and Kemp, Charles. *The Church and Community Resources*. St. Louis: Bethany Press, 1977.

Clinebell, Howard. *Basic Types of Pastoral Counseling*. Nashville: Abingdon Press, 1966.

Dale, Robert. *Growing a Loving Church: a Pastor's Guide to Christian Caring*. Nashville: Convention Press, 1974.

Hulme, William E. *The Pastoral Care of Families: Its Theology and Practice*. Nashville: Abingdon Press, 1974.

Kemp, Charles F. *A Pastoral Counseling Guidebook*. Nashville: Abingdon Press, 1971.

Oates, Wayne E. *An Introduction to Pastoral Counseling*. Nashville: Broadman Press, 1959.

Oates, Wayne E., and Rowatt, Wade. *Before You Marry Them*. Nashville: Broadman Press, 1976.

Rassieur, Charles L. *The Problem Clergymen Don't Talk About*. Philadelphia: Westminster Press, 1976.

Cassette Tapes

Clendinning, Pat. *Dealing with Difficult Church Members*. Nashville: Broadman Press, 1975.

Drakeford, John. *Helps for Divorcees*. Nashville: Broadman Press, 1974.

Madden, Myron. *Hospital Visitation*. Nashville: Broadman Press, 1974.

Marney, Carlyle. *How to Be a Human Being*. Nashville: Broadman Press, 1977.

Oates, Wayne. *A Guide to Counseling*. Nashville: Broadman Press, 1974.

Self, William. *How "Koinonia" Develops*. Nashville: Broadman Press, 1977.

8
Deacons as Family Ministers

A late-afternoon tornado swept through the area near the home of an elderly widow, a member of a city church. The deacon assigned to her in the family ministry plan of their church started immediately to see about her. After driving a few blocks, he found tree limbs and other debris blocking the streets. Turning back, he left his car at home and walked the mile or more to her home. The tornado had lifted just behind her house, and she was safe but extremely appreciative of his concern. She was also aware that, had the tornado struck her home, the deacon would have been there to do whatever was needed. This church, like many others, assigned each deacon a number of families for which he is responsible.

In Acts 6 we have the story of the early church confronting problems in ministering. The membership was made up of native-born Jewish people and of Jews who had come from Greek-speaking communities. Within the framework of the Jewish religion, widows had been cared for; so the new church followed that tradition. Daily ministry—the delivery of meals to homes of widows in need—was performed by the apostles.

With all the other responsibilities of the apostles, however, there was not adequate time to administer this program as carefully as was needed. Greek-speaking members of the church felt that Greek-speaking widows were being neglected.

It is interesting that their complaint was accompanied by a proposed solution. They suggested that the church elect seven men to assist the apostles.

The apostles and the church accepted the proposal and elected Stephen, Phillip, Prochorus, Nicanor, Timon, Parmenas, and Nicolaus. These seven men were ordained for the work for which they had been selected.

Many churches today have officers who trace their beginnings to this passage from Acts. These are called *deacons,* an English word taken from the Greek *diakonas,* which means servant or minister. In some churches the deacons serve as business managers or as boards of directors. However, many churches are asking the deacons to serve with the pastor to accomplish the pastoral ministries of the church.[1]

The pastoral ministry load today is overwhelming. The leadership, proclamation, and care roles are so demanding that the pastor, like the apostles, finds that some of his important ministries are being neglected. Deacons can help the pastors by sharing some of the pastoral ministry load. The deacon who visited following the tornado was assuming that role.

There are five areas in which deacons may contribute to the family ministry of the church. The first of these is in the area of listening. Really hearing what another has to say is one of the greatest affirmations one can give. The deacon who goes into a home to *tell* will miss opportunities for service which would have been found had he gone to *hear.* Sensitivity to need can be developed and is a part of the training of deacons in family ministry.

Deacons also minister in times of crisis. Illness, death, tragedies, and other crises come to the lives of every family. The deacon who has been close to the family will be aware of such crises. Having someone available during long hours at the bedside of a loved one, during loneliness following the funeral—during heartaches of any kind—can be comforting. By his presence and his words of comfort the deacon can help to lighten the load. He can help to bear the burden.

Sometimes, too, there is the need for practical help. Someone may be needed to help with funeral arrangements, with selecting and purchasing a burial plot, with probating a will, and other matters. The deacon may help in whatever ways he can and may make referrals when advisable.

Many persons need help in working through the grief process. The most valuable ministry may come in the weeks and months after the funeral, when the bereaved is guided through the process of accepting his loss, expressing his grief, and learning to live again. Children, too, need to be remembered during this period of grief.

Marital problems are another type of crisis occurring more and more often in today's society. Through listening and observation during visitation, deacons may become aware of marital problems and thus be able to help or to lead the couple to seek professional help.

Sometimes marital and family problems are not solved and divorce results. Nonjudgmental support from the deacon is needed at this time. Regardless of who is at fault or what the problem may be, each person involved in divorce—and that includes children of the couple and sometimes even their parents—needs love and acceptance. Divorced persons are sometimes treated as lepers, banished from Christian fellowship regardless of the circumstances. The supportive and affirming minsty of deacons can help persons involved in divorce from feeling rejected by the church.

Deacons may hear confessions of problems of almost any nature. Through their training they will learn to be accepting and nonjudgmental—not condoning but not condemning.

Many personal and family crises result from lack of growth or understanding of developmental needs. Deacons can be of tremendous help in interpreting and assisting with developmental stages of life. The crises of youth are often the result of conflict between parent and youth regarding his need for independence. Many parents want to hold on and completely control the youth. Youth yearn to be released to function as responsible individuals. Their rebellion may be demonstrated in a variety of ways. If the deacon has won the confidence of youth among the families to which he is assigned, he may be able to provide needed guidance for them.

The adult entering the middle years may have difficulties, and the family may have difficulties if the significance of this passage is not understood. Individual reading and group discussions in deacon training will help the deacon to become familiar with potential trouble areas in the life developmental cycle.

Another area in which the deacon may participate in family ministry is in the clarifying of biblical understandings of family relationships. The deacon will want to study carefully chapter 3, along with the suggestions for further study. He may find that many families are misinterpreting biblical passages, or he may find that they are ignoring them. Without being dogmatic or authoritarian, the deacon may share his concept of biblical teachings on the family. He may notify families of special studies or sermons relating to biblical teachings on family relationships. And he may also share with the pastor requests for special biblical teachings or sermons.

Within the membership of most churches, there are incomplete families. Dad may be a member of the church; Mother and the children may not be. Both parents may be in the church but children have never become Christians. Or a child may have come to church with neighbors and have become a part of the church membership, but his parents may not be Christians. As the deacon visits with the church member in the family, he will have an opportunity to witness to other members of the family who are not Christians or who are not a part of any church. As he cultivates the friendship of the entire family, the deacon will pray for God's guidance in his efforts to share his Christian faith with those who need Christ.

Families may be assigned to deacons geographically or alphabetically, depending on the community. A downtown city church—or any church scattered over a large geographical area—will likely find organization by geographical area easier. Assignment may be made for the length of the deacon's term of service (usually three years). Time is needed to establish a relationship, so annual assignments are not usually advisable. However, if there is a personality conflict or if a deacon feels he has not been able to establish a relationship with a family after a reasonable time, changes of assignment probably should be made. New families will be assigned to a deacon as they come into the fellowship.

The deacon chairman should organize the church membership into groups, assign groups to deacons, and lead in a program of training. He should also use whatever methods are available of notifying the church membership of the plan.

The chairman may choose to use a portion of each deacons' meeting for family ministry discussions. But he will likely rely on special activities, such as retreats, for at least part of the training and planning.

The deacon secretary is responsible for providing record books for each deacon. He will work with the deacon chairman in assigning groups and will receive reports from deacons each month, compile them, and submit them to the deacon chairman.

Each individual deacon may visit each assigned family regularly, communicating information concerning the church. He will visit and minister to families in crises and cooperate with the deacon chairman in all phases of family ministry assigned to him.

The Church Administration Department of the Baptist Sunday School Board provides resources for deacons to use in their visits in homes. Pamphlets relating to specific needs may be left in the home when appropriate.

Note

1. The Church Administration Department of The Sunday School Board of the Southern Baptist Convention has developed

a program known as The Deacon Family Ministry Plan. This chapter is based on that program.

For Further Study

Mosley, Ernest. "The Deacon Family Ministry Plan." Nashville: Convention Press, 1976.

9
The Family Serving

Service is an integral part of the Christian faith. Works are the expression of faith (Jas. 2:17), and the growing Christian family is one becoming rich in good works.

Church leaders are concerned with service from two perspectives. They want the work to be done. They see needs: the delinquent junior high girl, the lonely retiree, the grieving young widow, the couple on the verge of divorce, the newcomer, the youth on probation in a drugs case, the mentally ill, the man who is losing his self-respect because he cannot find a job, the foreign student, the college student away from home, the young mother tied down with a mentally retarded child, the wife and children of a convict—everywhere there are people with needs. Church leaders want to provide help in every such situation.

Leaders are also concerned that members of their congregations grow in their commitment to service. Leaders see themselves as equippers, but often feel their members are not ready and willing to be equipped. Existing organizations may not be able to assume all the loads; yet there is a fear that the church is already overorganized. Additional staff may seem to be the only solution, but often finances will not permit that approach. And there may be a better way.

Families are a logical service unit often overlooked by churches. Family members themselves have not often thought of the family as a unit of service. Instead, each member of the family may serve through other groups; and the family unit is fragmented. Dad and Mom visit for their Sunday School classes, and Dad works on a mission project with a men's group. Mom is involved in a mission action group, and each child serves with his age group. Seldom ever does the family work together in a service project.

Church leaders may be interested in leading families to become service-minded. Not only is the use of families an effective way of doing some aspects of the church's work, but it is an effective training approach for youth and children—and maybe parents, too.

The pastor's problem is leading persons to care. Church members must be led to see beyond buildings and budgets and organization and to recognize and respond to needs. What is the overall emphasis of the church? What do members consider to be "effective" church work? Are the amount of the budget and the number of baptisms the only measures of success? The pastor will have a great deal to do with the answers to these questions. He is usually the most influential person in determining the church's priorities.

The Family Praying

Intercessory prayer is one way in which a family may be led to serve together. Family prayer time often becomes a time when needs of each family member are shared and become objects of prayer. This experience is good and should be continued, but many families can be led to accept wider areas of concern. Not only will the causes for which they pray be blessed, but also the habit of intercessory prayer will be taught to children and youth in these families.

The following suggestions may be helpful for leaders to share with families:

• Let the entire family have a part in deciding on objects of prayer. A child may be asked to prepare a list of agreed-upon concerns. This list may be used as a prayer guide in each family worship session.

• Make prayer requests as specific as possible. "Bless all our missionaries" is not as meaningful as "Bless the Barnes in their work in Argentina today." "Bless the sick" will not mean as much as "Bless Mrs. Freeman and help her to get well if it is your will."

• Continue praying daily until the prayer is answered. "Help Mr. McDonald to find a job" or a prayer for the teenage neighbor on drugs may remain on the family prayer list until the time when thanksgiving for answered prayer is appropriate.

• Record dates of answered prayer. A prayer list with dates of answers becomes a contemporary version of Hebrews 11.

Pastors who know of families who use this approach or who may be encouraged to begin the practice may share with them additional requests from time to time. A telephone call from the pastor to the Blake family to share information and request prayer concerning a recently discovered need not only lightens the pastor's load, but also helps the Blakes to grow.

Families in Outreach

Families may also serve in outreach. These stories illustrate how churches may use families in reaching other families for Christ and the church.

The Robertses had new neighbors who had not become affiliated with any local church. The Robertses went far beyond a routine visit to invite the newcomers to their own church; they cultivated their friendship by inviting them to a backyard barbecue, by taking them to visit a local historical spot, and by introducing them to community services. These and many other types of activities helped establish relationships necessary for the most effective witnessing. Many families would accept such responsibility if it were suggested to them.

When ten-year-old Johnny is the only person in his family attending Sunday School, the family of one of his classmates may be asked to visit Johnny's home to seek to enlist other members of the family. When an entire family drops out of church, another family may be asked to visit to discover problems and to seek to help.

The Family Ministering

Families may also serve effectively as ministry units. The following will suggest other types of ministry which may be appropriate.

Sara, a single parent, lost her job. She found herself faced with the problem of finding a cheaper apartment, feeding her two children and herself, securing school clothes for her older child—and finding a new job.

The Wilson family—who had not known her previously—were asked by the church to come to her rescue. Ralph Wilson helped her in her contacts with public-housing authorities. Mrs. Wilson took Sara to the church for groceries from the church ministry pantry. Sara's ten-year-old was outfitted for school with clothes too small for the fast-growing Sam Wilson, and Mrs. Wilson found a neighbor who shared with Sara's preschooler clothes outgrown by her child.

When Sara went for a job interview, the Wilsons' teenage daughter sat with her children to save baby-sitting fees. The entire Wilson family became involved at the time of Sara's need. They cared. They grew through the experience, and Sara's courage and hope were kept alive.

There had been a death in the family of thirteen-year-old Kent. His father was the victim of a heart attack. His friend Ray's parents went to the funeral home and also took food to the home. They discovered that Kent's three-year-old brother was having a difficult time, so they offered to keep him for a few hours. They also discovered that Kent was uncomfortable at the funeral home. Like most boys his age, he did not know how to express his grief and did not know how to respond to the consolation offered by adults. Ray's parents felt that Kent would be more comfortable with friends of his own age around and suggested that Ray go for a visit. To prepare Ray for this ministry, they talked about how Kent must feel in the loss of his father and how it might help to have some of his friends with him. Ray was reluctant but finally agreed to be a part of the ministry to his friend at this time of need. The two boys went to Kent's room alone; and, although they probably were not completely at ease, the visit was helpful for the friend in need.

Why was this family so alert to need? Their pastor had recently led several prayer meeting discussions on ways families can minister in times of need. The pastor's secretary had called them to tell them that the father of Ray's friend had died.

At holiday times there are many lonely people who appreciate invitations and other attention. Retirement-home patients, internationals, children from orphanages, singles, recently widowed persons living alone—these often dread holiday seasons. Families may adopt one or more persons and entertain them in their homes. Church leaders may keep lists of persons who might appreciate such invitations and, upon request, share these names with families in the congregation. Care should be taken to see that the guest is not made to feel like a *project;* the effectiveness of the offer can be ruined by a thoughtlessly worded invitation. Families may give each child responsibility in planning for and entertaining the guest. The occasion may be as happy for the host family as for the guest.

Families may also minister to shut-ins who cannot be out for the holiday visits. Daily or weekly telephone calls, notes, surprise packages, and other ways of saying "we care" are meaningful. A family may adopt one shut-in and minister to him regularly, or they may remember a different one each week. A daily phone call to the elderly person who lives alone will be especially meaningful. Birthdays of shut-ins may become special times of remembrance by adopted families. When the family decorates their own Christmas tree, they may decorate another one to be taken to a shut-in or to a hospital. Valentine Day is a time to share love, perhaps by giving potted plants, cookies, or other small items. From time to time the entire family may visit for a worship time—Bible reading, prayer, and, if the family is musical, singing. Shut-ins who have no opportunity to attend worship services will especially appreciate this type of ministry. A teenager may tape the worship service and the family may participate in worship with the church.

Church leaders may want to insist that the mother not be solely responsible for the ministry, but that Dad and the children share in the phone calls, visits, notes, and other remembrances. The tendency in some families will be to leave it all to Mother.

The Family and New Churches

In the establishment of new churches, families often render a great service. Often parents are contacted rather than the entire family when such service is considered, however.

A family moved into a subdivision where there was no church. They were willing to drive the additional miles to attend their old church, but were aware that most of their neighbors were not attending church anywhere.

Their pastor asked the entire family to visit him in his study one day. He talked with them about the need for a church in their neighborhood and the interest of their church in sponsoring it. He asked if they would be willing to become the leaders in this venture. He especially emphasized the part of the teenagers; they would be leaving their friends in all the church activities and would have responsibility of helping start new groups, which might be a difficult task. Even the six-year-old was included. The pastor pointed out that he would not have a children's room with pretty furniture in the new church. He would not have a children's choir and some of the other things he especially enjoyed. The use of their home as a meeting place would involve each member of the family assuming some responsibility. The pastor pointed out that the mother should not be the one to get the breakfast dishes done, the beds made, and other Sunday morning chores necessary if a Sunday School was to meet in their home each Sunday. But the entire family would be helping to reach other families and, eventually, to start a new church. He asked them to think and pray as a family before they made their decision.

After a week or two, the family came back to the pastor offering their services and their home. A neighborhood Bible study began first. As it grew, a Sunday School was organized. After a year a new church was organized, a pastor called, a building rented, and plans made for construction of a permanent building.

The Family and Missions

Families may also be enlisted to conduct Backyard Bible Clubs. The church may agree to furnish materials for any family who will conduct a summer (or school vacation time) Bible club for neighborhood children for five afternoons or early evenings. Working parent can participate too when these clubs meet in early evenings. Preparation is not difficult; and in addition to having fun as a family, members can provide valuable teaching for children not in Sunday School.

A new area of family service is opening up in relation to mission work. Some families use their vacation time to serve in home or foreign mission projects. After an earthquake a building contractor and his wife, a home economist, served in reconstruction and in feeding volunteer workers. A doctor and his wife, a nurse, and their teenagers served in a mission hospital while missionaries had a few days to rest. Families may help take a religious census and conduct Vacation Bible Schools in areas where churches are needed. Many skills are needed on both home and foreign mission fields, and family life will be enriched as family members share their services. Information concerning needs for volunteers may be secured from the mission boards.

Leading Families to Serve

What is the handle for church leaders to use in promoting service by families? There are several options.

The pulpit is the most obvious. The pastor may preach one or more sermons on the family as ministers. He may give practical suggestions for response.

A series of studies in this area might be held on Wednesday or Sunday evenings. A setting other than a worship service may be the most effective.

The informal approach will probably be best; but for those who want more structure, a workshop approach may be used.

Family groups may be asked to sit together during such a workshop and may be asked to suggest ideas. The leader may present the needs (by type rather than by names of persons) and ask for brainstorming on ways families may meet needs. Each family group may then be asked to discuss together ways they can serve. Commitment cards may be used if desired.

```
┌─────────────────────────────────────────────┐
│        Family Service Commitment            │
│     We agree as a family to serve our Lord in the │
│  following ways:                            │
│  _____│
│  _____│
│  Signed_____│
│  _____│
│  _____│
└─────────────────────────────────────────────┘
```

Be sure to insist that each member of the family sign the commitment card. Cards may be collected for follow-through, or they may be kept by the family as a reminder of their agreement.

Follow-through will be important to make the activity most useful. From time to time a family may be asked to share a testimony of some experience they have had. The group (families participating in the initial meeting) may agree to meet monthly or quarterly to share experiences. Church leaders may provide through the media center training materials which will be helpful in ministering in various types of situations. If there is a need, short-term training groups may be set up. Include all the family in these training groups.

From time to time a church leader may telephone involved families to ask for a progress report or to share experiences. This will take time from the church leaders' schedule—but the family will be assuming a great deal of responsibility formerly carried by the leaders themselves.

The danger in structured approaches is that they

may become too mechanical. This danger may be avoided by maintaining spontaneity and flexibility in family service projects.

Families can become service oriented. Church leaders are the key to enlistment, commitment, and training.

For Further Study

Bingham, Robert. *A Cup of Cold Water.* Nashville: Convention Press, 1971.

Mission Action Group Guide: Aging. Birmingham: Woman's Missionary Union, 1972.

Mission Action Group Guide: Child Care. Birmingham: Woman's Missionary Union, 1969.

Mission Action Group Guide: Economically Disadvantaged. Birmingham: Woman's Missionary Union, 1967.

Mission Action Group Guide: Headliners. Birmingham: Woman's Missionary Union, 1969.

Mission Action Group Guide: Internationals. Birmingham: Woman's Missionary Union, 1967.

Mission Action Group Guide: The Sick. Birmingham: Woman's Missionary Union, 1967.

Thomason, William O. *The Life Givers.* Nashville: Broadman Press, 1973.

Appendix

Programs

The following are programs and recommendations for various types of family ministry meetings. Church leaders may find suggestions and ideas to help in their own planning.

Family Life Conference

Sunday
  Sunday School hour
    9:40 A.M. "Making Your Marriage Succeed"
    All Adults—Auditorium
  Morning Worship
    11:00 A.M. "The Elbow Ministry"
  Church Training hour
    6:00 P.M. "The Generation Gap"
    All Adults—Auditorium
  Evening Worship
    7:00 P.M. "What Makes a Home Christian"
    8:00 P.M. "How to Keep from Making a Mess of Things"
    Youth Fellowship hour—Fellowship Hall
Monday
    7:00 P.M. "Enemies of the Home"

7:40 P.M.   Conference
"Changing Roles of Husbands and Wives"
8:30 P.M.   Adjourn

Tuesday
12:00 P.M.   Luncheon (Retirement and above)
7:00 P.M.   "Communicating Love"
7:40 P.M.   Conference
"Meeting Needs of One-parent Families"
8:30 P.M.   Adjourn

Wednesday
5:30 P.M.   Family Supper
6:15 P.M.   Regular Organizational Meetings
7:00 P.M.   "Crowning Christ Through the Home"
7:40 P.M.   Adjourn

Single Adult Retreat

Friday Evening
5:00–8:00 P.M.   Registration and Room Assignment
6:00 P.M.   Supper for those with supper reservations
7:30 P.M.   Getting Acquainted and Program Orientation
8:00 P.M.   Worship Period
9:00 P.M.   Talent Time
9:45 P.M.   Adjourn for the evening

Saturday Morning
7:30 A.M.   Morning Watch (Beach Service)
8:00 A.M.   Breakfast
9:00 A.M.   Personal Growth Seminars:
1.   Leadership Conference
2.   "The Challenge of Being Single"

    3.   "Personal Financing for Singles"
    4.   "Living as a Single Parent" (personal problems)
    5.   "Developing the Dimensions of Intimacy"
    6.   "Building Self-esteem"

10:15 A.M.   Refreshment Break
10:45 A.M.   SYMPOSIUM: "Programs and Activities for Singles"
12:15 P.M.   Lunch

Saturday Afternoon

1:15 P.M.   "Sexuality and the Single"
2:30 P.M.   Free Time
5:30 P.M.   Supper

Saturday Evening

6:30 P.M.   Personal Growth Seminars:
    1.   "Living as a Single Parent" (parenting problems)
    2.   "Developing the Dimensions of Intimacy"
    3.   "Building Self-esteem"
    4.   "Coping with Boredom"

7:45 P.M.   "Learning to Love—or Love Again"
8:30 P.M.   "The Right to Marry—or Remarry"
9:15 P.M.   Break; Small-group Rap Sessions
10:00 P.M.   You may want to go eat again!

Sunday Morning

8:00 A.M.   Breakfast
9:00 A.M.   Bible Study
10:00 A.M.   Morning Worship
11:30 A.M.   Lunch—Depart for home or stay at leisure

Family Life/Single Life Conference

Friday
> 7:00 P.M.   Banquet for Adults and Youth
> "Communicating Love"
> 8:00 P.M.   Choice of Conferences
> Singles: "You Are Not the Other Half of the Apple"
> Adults and Youth: "The Generation Gap"

Saturday
> 8:00 A.M.   Men's Breakfast
> Prepurchased Ticket $1
> "The Role of the Man in the Home"
> 9:30 A.M.   Coffee for Parents
> "The Pleasure and Problems of Preteens"
> 11:00 A.M.   Coffee for the Ladies
> "The Role of the Woman in the Home"
> 4:00 P.M.   Choice of Conferences
> "The Single Life"
> "Coping with Being Single Again"
> 5:00 P.M.   Snack Supper—by Reservation—$1
> 6:00 P.M.   "Questions Often Asked by Singles"
> Single Again
> Single
> 7:30 P.M.   Choice of Conferences
> "Marriage Enrichment"
> "What Parents Should Teach About Sex"

Sunday
> 9:45 A.M.
> Couples: "Making Your Good Home Better"
> Singles: "Should You Consider Marriage or Remarriage?"

Single Adult Retreat

Friday Evening
    5:30 P.M.   Faculty Dinner
    6:30–8:30 P.M. Registration
    8:00 P.M.   "Touching Hands" (group fellowship time)
    8:20 P.M.   "A Meridian Welcome"
    8:30 P.M.   Theme Music Interpretation
      "Lessons from a Bible Single"
    9:00 P.M.   *Touch Life Conferences* (Choose one)
    1. "In Touch with My Feelings"
    2. "I Love Me" (building self-esteem)
    3. "Touching Shoulders" (building dimensions of friendship)
    4. "Courting Couples' Communication"
    5. "Understanding Sexuality"
    6. "Excess Baggage—How to Unload It"
    10:30 P.M. Friendship and Prayer Group

Saturday
    7:30 A.M. Breakfast (at your discretion)
    8:30 A.M. Theme Music Interpretation
    9:30 A.M. "Who Are We? What Are We Doing in the Churches?"
    9:50 A.M. Refreshment Break
    10:10 A.M. "Coping With Being Single Again"
      (For those single again up to 3 years)
      "Coping With Being Single Again"
      (For those single again more than three years)
      "Christian Single Life-style"
      (For never-marrieds)

"Leading Single Adults"
(For Single adult leadership)

11:10 A.M.   *Touch Life Conferences* (Choose a different one)

Continuation of the Leadership Conference

12:15 noon   Buffet Fellowship Luncheon

1:15 P.M.   Theme Music Interpretation
"Lessons from a Bible Single"

1:45 P.M.   *Touch Life Conferences* (Choose another)

Continuation of the Leadership Conference

2:45 P.M.   *Free Time*—or you may choose to attend a conference for single parents, "One Parent Serving as Two"

5:30 P.M.   *Touch Life Conferences* (Choose another)

6:30 P.M.   Fellowship Supper
Music Entertainment
"Reach Out and Touch"

8:30 P.M.   Some will be going home.

For Those Who Stay Over Saturday Night:

Sunday

8:30–9:30 A.M.   "Sunday Morning Afterglow"—Sunday School lesson
"He Touched Me"
(Fellowship in Sharing)

A Christian Marriage Enrichment Retreat

Friday

6:30–7:30 P.M.   Dinner

7:30–10:00 P.M. A. The Retreat Convenant
                        B. "Getting to know you, getting to know all about you"
                        C. The Logos of Marriage

10:00–? "Re-Creation"

Saturday

8:30–9:30 A.M. Breakfast

9:30–10:30 A.M. "Keeping Your Marriage in Shape"

10:30–10:45 A.M. Break

10:45–12:00 A.M. "Selfishness and Self-love in Christ"

12:00–1:00 P.M. Lunch

1:00–4:00 P.M. Free Time

4:30–6:00 P.M. "Loving Your Mate as Yourself"

6:00–7:00 P.M. Dinner

7:30–8:45 P.M. "Intimacy and Individuality in Marriage"

8:45–9:00 P.M. Break

9:00–10:00 P.M. "Creative Conflicts"

10:00–? "Re-Creation"

Sunday

8:30–9:30 A.M. Breakfast

9:30–11:00 A.M. "A Time to Share, Care, and Covenant"

11:00–12:00 A.M. Marriage Enrichment Worship Service—
                      "The Celebration of Faithfulness"

12:00–1:00 P.M. Lunch

7:30–8:30 P.M. Sunday Night Worship Service at the Home Church

What Is a Better Homes Club?

(some thoughts and suggestions from the pastor)

Purpose: The purpose of a Better Homes Club is to strengthen the family life within our congregation and community and provide a stimulus for personal and family development. The club would not be group therapy for "sick" marriages, but rather a means of strengthening good marriages by opening new avenues of communication and dialogue.

Programs: The Better Homes Club would meet eight to twelve times a year for dinner to discuss relevant topics that have bearing upon our lives today. A resource speaker would be invited to address the club with adequate time following his talk for discussion. The entire membership of the club would assist in choosing the topics for the progams. Some possible subjects include:

The Male Animal	How to Keep the Romance Alive
The Female Animal	
Inlaws or Outlaws	Raising a Family
How to Fight Fair	The Role of Fatherhood/ Motherhood
Religion in the Home	
Sterility and Fertility	Sex Education for Young People
Psychosexual Development of Children	
	Family Finances
Teenage Problems	Coping with the Drug Culture
Public-school Education	
Buying a Home	New Life-styles in the Home
Insuring Your Family	
Legal Aspects of Marriage	Adjustments in Marriage

The Problem of Older Parents

Dishes, Diapers, and Daddies

The Jewish Concept of the Home

Love in Marriage

The New Morality

Prejudice

Religious Training in the Home

Teenage Rebellion and Fads

Mental Mechanisms and

Mental Illness

Who Am I?

Winds of Change in the Protestant Church

New Direction in Religious Education

Bridging the Generation Gap

The Games Couples Play

Women's Lib and the Home

The Art of Intimacy

Will, Trusts, and the Future

Officers: The offices would be held by husband and wife and could include the following:

1. President
2. Vice-President
3. Secretary-treasurer
4. Food Chairman
5. Child Care
6. Publicity Chairman
7. Decoration Chairman
8. Hospitality Chairman

Child Care: A very big thing! We would need to make arrangements for children birth through preschool or the third grade for every meeting.

Well, what do you think? Does this sound like something you would be interested in? An initial dinner meeting is scheduled.

The Tender Loving Care Committee

This committee works with the minister of pastoral care to:

A. Telephone, visit, or send a card to a homebound member of the church family on a weekly or monthly basis as is appropriate. This is an adopt-a-person program.

B. Send cards to the people on the weekly prayer list of the church.

C. The emergency care ministry provides transportation to doctors, hospitals, grocery stores, and so forth. They also stay with hospital patients or homebound members so that the family of those members can go home, shopping, and so forth. The people in this ministry will provide special services such as transportation or grocery shopping for short-term periods of time.

D. The rest home ministry provides for weekly or monthly visits to a church member in a Rest Home. It is done in cooperation with the special ministries subcommittee of the mission committee, which provides for worship services and Bible studies in the rest homes. This is an adopt-a-person program. This committee is also coordinated with the deacon flock program.

Spiritual Growth Retreats for Couples

The *Spiritual Growth Retreats* are for young couples recently married (first two years) because they do not know their mates well enough—nor have they had to face enough developmental tasks in marriage adjustment—for the typical marriage enrichment retreat to be as beneficial as with couples married longer.

This emphasis upon sharing their spiritual pilgrimage is less threatening, awakens the cutting edges of spiritual growth for each person, provides for a reemphasis that God is the head of the marriage relationship, encourages a communication of sharing between mates that relates to the ultimate questions and meanings of life, models possible meaningful and practical religious rituals in the home, and builds a community of friend couples to be a support system during a very important time of marital adjustment.

Dedication of Parents

Pastor: For blessing our home with the joys of parenthood, we declare our partnership with our creator, as . . .

Parents: We express deep gratitude to God for this child.

Pastor: Knowing that God has a plan for the life of each person he creates and that our influence as Christian parents will largely effect the fulfillment of that plan . . .

Parents: We ask God's continuing guidance in nurturing our child.

Pastor: Realizing that his will must have first place, we want to recognize him daily in our home and determine to combine Bible reading and prayer with Christian example, as . . .

Parents: We commit ourselves to the teaching of Christian values each day.

Pastor: Knowing that the church family joins earnestly in the endeavor to give our child Christian training, we are happy for them to share in the joy of guiding this little one to know Jesus' love and care, as . . .

Parents: We pledge to raise our child in the church.

Pastor: Because we assume the responsibility of spiritual training, as well as providing means of physical, mental and social development . . .

Parents: We consecrate our own lives anew to Christ, as we seek to establish a home that is genuinely Christian.

Recommendations

We recommend that:

I. A *family life committee* of six persons be established to advise the pastor and minister of pastoral care regarding:

  A. The annual Christian family life education emphasis

  B. The enrichment retreats and Christian growth groups for individuals, couples, and families

  C. The integration of Christian family life education into the ongoing educational program

  D. Ministry training

  E. A referral system

  F. Policy related to the counseling ministry.

  This committee would be nominated by the nominating committee and elected by the church.

II. A sliding scale fee be set up for in-depth, multiple-interview pastoral counseling for people who are not members of the church. (Some churches charge counseling fees because they believe counselees take sessions more seriously if they pay. Other churches do not charge for counseling.) These are people usually referred to the pastors by other professional persons. They suffer from deep inner conflicts with values that may concretely relate to personal adjustments, marital relationships, or family relationships in which they do not want to do what they want to do (Rom. 7:15). The fee would (1) apply to all interviews after the initial interview, and (2) its purpose would be to determine whether the person(s) is serious in wanting to deal with the broken relationships (sin) in his life.

III. The pastors be allowed to make covenants of responsibility with church members who come and who are in need of in-depth, multiple-interview pastoral counseling. This is different from and more complex than the other levels of pastoral care. The other levels include *friendship, comfort* such as in bereavement, *admission of guilt* over past sins so that forgiveness may be realized, *teaching* which would include premarital guidance, and *brief pastoral dialogues* in which the pastor serves as an aid to the decision-making process.

People who need counseling are already experiencing such a sense of failure that they should not be put into a position where all they can do is receive ministry (charity) from the counselor. As ministry through counseling is received by them, the covenant of responsibility would involve their choosing to minister to someone else. This could be (1) a commitment to change behavior toward another person in their family, (2) a commitment to serve in some position of service at church, or (3) a commitment to minister to another person(s) in a concrete way. It would be only as a last resort that the person would be allowed to give a limited sum in return for receiving counseling. The emphasis here is that the counselee chooses to *do* something as a sign of taking the counseling seriously.

However, there is an even greater spiritual dimension involved in the covenant the counselee makes. It is only as each counselee accepts the areas of his own degree of responsibility for a broken relationship that progress can be made. Yet confessing one's own sins is seldom sufficient atonement for bad behavior. It must usually be followed by a literal or symbolic act of restitution in order for realized forgiveness to be experienced and future behavior changed.

The conditions of the covenant of responsibility would vary according to the unique situation and the mutual agreement between each counselee and counselor. Any disclosure of the conditions would be done only after consulting all parties involved in the covenant.

IV. Any monies received in the counseling ministry will be put in a special fund administered by the family life committee. This money would be used as necessary to share the expenses when a counselee was referred to a psychiatrist, psychologist, lawyer, doctor, or other professional person. This would be based upon the recommendation of the pastor or minister of pastoral care. The money would be used for consultation with a professional person by one of the pastors only upon mutual agreement between the pastors and the family life committee.

FAMILY ENRICHMENT SERIES BOOKS 1977
(Published by Convention Press)

SENIOR ADULTS—*Life in the Senior Years*
ADULTS—*Staying in the Black Financially*
OLDER YOUTH—*$: a Handbook on Money for Youth*
YOUNGER YOUTH—*Dad, About My Allowance*
OLDER CHILDREN—*If I Had a Money Tree*
YOUNGER CHILDREN—*My Family's Money*
PRESCHOOLERS—*My Family and Our Church*

FAMILY ENRICHMENT SERIES BOOKS 1978

SINGLE PARENTS—*Helps for the Single-Parent Christian Family*
COUPLES—*Christian Marriage: Games or Growth?*
OLDER YOUTH—*There's No Place Like Home?!*
YOUNGER YOUTH—*Home, Sweet(?), Home*
OLDER CHILDREN—*Adventures in Family Living*
YOUNGER CHILDREN—*Growing Up in My Family*
PRESCHOOLERS—*My Family Loves Me*

FAMILY ENRICHMENT SERIES BOOKS 1979

SENIOR ADULTS—*Hooray for Grandparents!*
SINGLE ADULTS—*Thirty Plus and Single*
PARENTS—*How to Prepare Your Children for Marriage*
OLDER YOUTH—*Together? You and Me?*
YOUNGER YOUTH—*About This Thing Called Dating*
OLDER CHILDREN—*What Makes Christian Families Special?*
YOUNGER CHILDREN—*What Are Families For?*
PRESCHOOLERS—*Having Fun at Home*